# Glimpses of Calgary Past

## by Jean Leslie

Detselig Enterprises Ltd.

Calgary, Alberta, Canada

**Glimpses of Calgary Past**
© 1994 Jean Leslie

Canadian Cataloguing in Publication Data

Leslie, Jean, 1920 -
  Glimpses of Calgary Past

  ISBN 1-55059-099-5

  1. Calgary (Alta.)--History. 2. Calgary (Alta.)--Biography

  I. Title.
  FC3697.4.L47 1994        971.23'38        C94-910826-X
  F1079.5.C35L47 1994

Detselig Enterprises Ltd.
Suite 210, 1220 Kensington Road, N.W.
Calgary, Alberta   T2N 3P5
Canada

Publisher's Caution

Most of the information contained herein was obtained by personal interviews by the author. Some facts may not agree with currently accepted historical accounts. While every effort has been made to ensure accuracy, the publisher accepts no responsibility for historical innaccuracies. Detselig Enterprises Ltd. will gladly accept information that clarifies any reference or credit.

The majority of these stories were edited from their previously printed forms that appeared primarily in the *Calgary Herald* newspaper and various local magazines.

Cover Design by Dean MacDonald

Printed in Canada        ISBN 1-55059-099-5        SAN 115-0324

*To the pioneers
who laid the foundation
for the great city that is Calgary.*

# Acknowledgements

I wish to express my deep appreciation to my brother Rob Logan and my sister Ferrol Logan who helped with computer work. To Douglas McArthur of Script: the Writer's Group and Elizabeth Longmore of More Communications, for their advice and encouragement; to Pat Molesky for her help at the Glenbow Museum's picture archives; to Margaret Fraser, Joan Langford and Bill Tidball of the Historical Committee for the Calgary Exhibition and Stampede; to Mayor Duerr and Ron Esch for their support. To all who gave of their time for interviews.

And to my husband Jack, for his valuable input and his support.

\*\*\*\*\*

Detselig Enterprises Ltd. appreciates the financial support of our 1994 publishing program, provided by the Department of Canadian Heritage, Canada Council and the Alberta Foundation for the Arts, a beneficiary of the Lottery Fund of the Government of Alberta.

We wish to extend additional thanks to the Calgary Real Estate Board Co-Operative Ltd. for their financial assistance towards the preparation of the material for this book.

# Contents

✳✳✳✳✳

# *Preface*

The year 1994 is a very special one for Calgarians as it represents our Centennial of incorporation as a city. The year-long celebrations that have been planned take their root in the very communities that have both grown up with Calgary and will become an integral part of its future. In many ways, it's a celebration for which we have already spent 100 years preparing.

As one of the many exciting projects of our Centennial year, this project captures the true spirit of the celebration – the people, events, and attributes that make Calgarians proud of their city. The book includes a collection of unique stories about fascinating Calgary characters – some well known and some less well known individuals who have guided the development of Calgary.

Al Duerr
Mayor

# Photo Credits

With the exception of the author's personal photographs, and where otherwise indicated below, all pictures that appear in the text are from Calgary's Glenbow Museum Archives.

# Buildings Change, Memories Linger

*I*n the summer of 1928 I stood wide-eyed with wonder on the corner of Calgary's 17th Avenue and 4th Street West and thought this surely must be the busiest intersection in the world. I was just seven years old and fresh from the small central Alberta village of Rimbey where the most popular conveyance was still the horse and buggy. But on this corner dozens of cars whizzed by and street cars rattled around the corner (after the conductor got out and performed some magic with a long steel pole he poked into the tracks). I was allowed to walk to this busy corner by myself because I could get there without crossing any streets from my family's rooming house on 18th Avenue between 4th and 5th Streets. Calgary was suffering what seems to be a perennial disease – a housing shortage – so Mother, Daddy, and my four younger siblings and myself were squeezed into one room at Mrs. Legge's rooming house. We had fun with our landlady's name. "Does Mr. Foot know where Mrs. Legge is going?" Or, "I wonder if Mrs. Hand is doing the washing?" and we'd double up with laughter. We considered overcrowding a small price to pay for our entertainment.

It wasn't long before we had some ammunition for "one-upmanship" over other kids on the block. Our dad was working for Brotherston Electric, the firm which installed Calgary's first movietone and vitaphone talking picture equipment at the Capitol Theatre. The fact that Daddy was

*Logan Family, 1928. Top left to right: Aunt, Mother,*
*Rob, Joyce, myself. Bottom: Ila, cousin, Shirley.*

the accountant and knew nothing about electronics was beside the point.

It is hard for me to realize that the thousands who have come to Calgary since 1972 (when the theatre was demolished to make room for the Scotia Centre) never knew the glory of the old Capitol. Movie houses were built like palaces in the 1920s and the Capitol was no exception. A glittering marquee shone with so many lights you could stand there and warm yourself on a blustery winter's night, as I did. The foyer, attended by liveried and lovely usherettes, was roped off with thick purple velvet ropes; magnificent chandeliers dimmed as the massive velvet curtains parted. The first picture with the new equipment was *Mother Knows Best* and although it was not a talkie from start to finish, the principal parts of the dialogue were spoken. The music of the 125-piece New York Roxy Theater Orchestra reproduced on the movietone played to accompany the picture instead of a local pianist.

Old timers shook their heads and sadly noted that Calgary was losing local color when construction began on the million dollar Timothy Eaton Store, wiping out the billboards on the corner of 8th Avenue and 4th Street behind which native Indians had for years cooked their meals over campfires during city shopping expeditions. Also wiped out were the Chinese market gardens, and Chinese laundry shops where you might pick up not only your underwear and shirts but the odd buck on a gambling game. To play the game the proprietor dabbed black ink on your choice of characters printed on a paper. If you had enough dabs showing when a master paper with holes in it was put in place, you won. This Chinese game was the forerunner of the popular Keno now played in Las Vegas.

It was during the hot summer of 1928 that Calgarians realized the truth of the old saying "You never miss the water till the well runs dry." The old reservoir on the Bow River, main source of the city's water supply, became so low it was impossible to pump any water at all in some districts. During the previous winter delicate shreds of frozen vapor has cluttered the intake screen. A severe flood the next spring and a typhoid scare in the summer precipitated a decision to build Glenmore Dam which was, according to my Dad Leslie, too close to the city and on the wrong river!

The muggy heat made us glad to leave Mrs. Legge's one room for a two-bedroom duplex on 11th Avenue West. Gone, is the duplex and the cottage next door where our neighbor grew mushrooms in his basement. Some day, he was certain, people would eat mushrooms all year round. Everyone nodded sympathetically but knew full well that mushrooms were a summer treat found only in country pastures. He would not be deterred so, while his wife supported the family be teaching, he had loads of well-rotted manure dumped in his back yard and, mole-like, trundled it into the basement under cover of night. He sold the meagre crop of mushrooms to the Palliser Hotel where the privileged could enjoy their delicate flavor, even in winter.

Calgarians have been sports-conscious from the day in 1886 when Colonel McLeod formed his first curling club. In 1928 interest centred on baseball. Traffic came to a standstill as a huge crowd of men jammed 1st Street West to watch the game-play on a gigantic baseball diamond. *The Calgary Herald* had set up a notice board to show the World Series as the Yankees played the Cardinals. Play on the board was synchronized with a play-by-play description over loud speakers from *The Herald's* radio room which had a direct line to the stadium. Although we did not own a radio, that marvelous medium was just coming into its own in Calgary with W. W. Grant's *Voice of the Prairies* on which Cy Ebeneezer and the Kid fiddled out quadrilles and polkas.

At 12 storeys, the Palliser Hotel qualified as a real skyscraper. Just before school in September, mother took me downtown where we were simply overwhelmed at the height of the Palliser – eight floors and they were busy adding four more! Today it is almost lost among the modern skyscrapers. The purpose of our downtown expedition was to visit Osborne's Book Store to buy books, scribblers, erasers and pencils. We were no sooner in the store than a beautiful pencil box caught my eye. It was a double-decker made of wood. The top half swivelled on a hinge off the bottom to reveal more pencils and an eraser. The top, painted with flowers, was a sliding panel that clicked neatly in and out of its grooved slot. How I longed for it. After buying the necessities and calculating there was enough left for new school shoes, I coaxed mother into buying the pencil box.

No doubt Calgary felt pretty sophisticated in that year of 1928 but bread, milk, laundry and ice deliveries were still made with the original kind of horse power, and to accommodate the faithful animals the City still provided six watering troughs! In September, as I skipped off to Sunalta Cottage School with my precious pencil box clutched in my hand, I just knew that living in the big city of Calgary was going to be a great adventure. It has been. And now, 66 years later I would like to share some of the stories of the people I have met and places I have seen along the way.

✳ ✳ ✳ ✳ ✳

# Flying Ace Fred McCall

*I*n the middle of Calgary's Stampede Week in 1919 excitement was running high. Those packed in the Grandstand were vicariously enjoying the thrill of bronco riding and motor car racing. Everyone was waiting with spine-tingling anticipation for a Curtiss bi-plane scheduled to take off from centre field. Most excited were the two young sons of Stampede general manager E. L. Richardson, who had persuaded their father to let them go flying. Captain Fred McCall soon appeared, goggles perched on his forehead, and strode toward the spiderweb of slats and struts accompanied by the two boys who clambered happily into the front cockpit.

The deafening whine of the racing cars that were jockeying for positions on the racetrack (which surrounded the infield) was soon drowned out by an ear-splitting roar as the mechanic swung the plane's propeller and the engine burst to life.

The plane raced toward the west end of the field, rose about 200 feet and suddenly, the engine power failed. A collective gasp went up from the Grandstand as the audience realized McCall's only choices were to crash into the racing cars or look for a soft spot on the midway. He chose the latter. The plane bounced off a telephone pole and, carrying a festoon of wire, perched down on the roof of the nearby merry-go-round.

As luck would have it the ride was idle. The wide frame of the carousel held the plane like a bird on her nest. The passengers and engine were intact, only the propeller blades and outer shell were damaged. Fred McCall was a hero. But it was not the first time.

*McCall's crash landing onto the merry-go-round, 1919*

In 1916 Frederick Robert Gordon McCall of Calgary enlisted in the 175th Battalion CEF as a private soldier. He was 21, short, slight of build and dark-haired with a boyish grin which spread from ear to ear. He studied intensely at the Sarcee Military Camp located west of the city and earned his sergeant's stripes before going overseas.

Soon after arriving in England he was transferred to the flying school at Tadcaster in Yorkshire and graduated in December 1917. His first flights were reconnaissance missions over enemy lines, piloting what the airforce called "flying coffins"– heavy, slow, two-seater RE 8s. The German fighters in their swift fighter planes loved them –

"sitting ducks" they thought. True to his orders not to go looking for fights, in his first brush with the enemy Freddy headed for home.

But the Germans had other ideas. While one got on his tail, the other tried to shoot him down from above. They fired hundreds of rounds at his plane, but McCall out-maneuvered them, even with his cumbersome ship. As the enemy wasn't playing by his rules, Freddy decided he might as well play by theirs. He dived at one and, with his machine-guns blazing, shot one of them down. The other turned and fled.

This action, following in the wake of excellent work done on artillery patrols, resulted in Freddy McCall garnering the Military Cross. His second victory came just two days later while on a photographic patrol. He was attacked by a German flying an Albatross Scout. Instead of heading back for his own lines, McCall turned to meet the German head-on with a burst of machine-gun fire which hit the astonished German right "amidships." The plane crashed at terrific speed. In the same month McCall engaged a Rempler two-seater, and although his RE 8 was slow compared to it, he killed the observer, wounded the pilot and this plane crashed too. When he had added six more German planes to his list he was awarded a bar to his Military Cross. Following the announcement he was given two weeks leave in London and on April 25, 1918, he appeared before His Majesty King George V who pinned the Military Cross and bar to his tunic at an investiture at Buckingham Palace.

By now the authorities realized that if McCall could shoot down all those planes while piloting a clumsy RE 8, he must have better than average flying ability. In May 1918, he was transferred to the famous 41st Squadron of fighters equipped with SE 5s, the finest single engine fighter planes in the Royal Air Force. During the month of May he shot down three German planes, but he reached his peak the following month when no less than 16 planes fell to his guns in 31 days. And on June 30, 1918 he equalled the record of the famous Canadian pilot Billy Bishop by shooting down five in one day. He was made a member of the Distinguished Service Order (DSO), another honor to his growing list of accomplishments. During his greatest record of successes, McCall teamed up with another brilliant flier, Captain W.G. Claxton, DSO, DFC and between the two of them they cleared the air of German planes in their part of the Western Front.

*Captain Fred McCall with his JN-4, 1919*

Late in August, when out on a mission, McCall and Claxton were attacked by 40 German planes. They managed to bring down six of them before Claxton was shot down and taken prisoner. The tremendous strain began to take its toll on Freddy. Soon after, he was given three months leave of absence whereupon he returned to Calgary where he was when Armistice was signed.

How could Calgarians not be proud of him? Captain Fred McCall DSO, MC, DFC received top billing at the 1919 Victory Stampede. Still short and dark, but now with a tiny pot belly, Freddy settled down to "regular life," if you can use that expression when speaking of a barnstorming pilot. The month before the Victory Stampede he was down in Minneapolis inspecting the two powerful Curtiss bi-planes which he was to fly at the Stampede. They were doubly braced throughout for stunt flying and capable of what was then the amazing speed of 70 miles an hour!

It was widely publicized that his wife went with him and became the first Canadian woman and probably the first woman on the American continent who had gone through all the stunt flying known to aviation at that time. Captain McCall was quoted at the time as saying, "I hadn't gone up 50 feet the last time, until Mrs. McCall was asking me to do loop-the-loop. Why, down in Minneapolis the ladies invariable go up first and then if they like it, their husbands go up!" They did in Calgary too – my mother flew with him, paying only a cent per pound. At 100 pounds she got a bargain – $1 for her flight. As McCall's regular fare was only 3 cents a pound per passenger, it was going to take a lot of flights to make him any money, so he jumped at the chance to be a featured event at the Calgary Exhibition and Stampede to garner more publicity for his business.

\* \* \*

It was after several days of accident-free stunting that McCall had the accident I described earlier. As the bystanders rushed over to examine the plane and the merry-go-round they concluded Freddy had deliberately chosen that spot as the safest to land. With his war record it was easy to believe.

The wrecked plane was quickly dismantled, loaded onto a flat car and shipped to the Edmonton Exhibition where thousands of Edmontonians paid 50 cents apiece to see the remains of what was acclaimed across the country as *"The World's Most Unique Air Accident."*

McCall made the headlines, something he was to do often in the next few years as he tried everything imaginable to promote flying.

*"First non-stop trip from Calgary to Vancouver over the tops of the highest mountains – McCall hopes to cross Rockies by plane in spring"*, proclaimed *The Calgary Herald* on January 1, 1920.

McCall did it too.

Next he tried to make rain. *The Herald* in a story on March 19, 1920 pronounced *"Captain McCall will make an attempt to induce rain to fall this summer at the first favorable opportunity."* There was a Drought Relief Fund in Calgary in those days but that was a drop in the bucket compared to the need of farmers who were suffering crop losses. Small wonder that the populace was receptive to McCall's offer. His plan was based on a study already tested in South Africa. It was believed that dust, having come from earth, would have its full complement of electrons and by coming in contact with water molecules, the molecules would arrange themselves around the dust motes causing moisture to form and make rain. McCall's revolutionary proposal was to ascend above the cloud carrying with a him a quantity of sand or dust and scatter it through the cloud. Fortunately for the farmers, and perhaps for Freddy, moisture in the Summer of 1920 was abundant and his theory went untested. However, my husband Jack remembered that the theory was still around in the 1960s when he was an alderman and Calgary City Council voted funds to "seed the clouds" turning hail clouds into rain clouds. It did in fact work. It was tried up around Beiseker. But it was expensive and limited and therefore was not continued.

In 1919 McCall founded the first Calgary-based aircraft company and in 1927, the Calgary Aero Club. But these new businesses didn't stop him from still doing crazy stunts. My friend Don Patterson, who later became a Second World War pilot, remembered he and his father took off with Freddy from the airstrip behind Stanley Jones School in a ski-equipped Curtiss Robin, and landing at Banff went on by a dog-sled team to Mount Assiniboine. He even remembered seeing "ski-joring" behind a plane (this was usually done with a car or horse). "McCall would have a really long rope – 100 to 200 feet long, long enough to avoid the prop wash. Then he'd tow along the skier. They would do about 40 or 50 miles an hour – a hell of a speed for a skier in those days!"

Another of my friends, Jack Peach, lived right across the street from his idol. "We ate, slept and lived aviation with McCall and not only was he my hero but he was a source of income – I regularly washed his Chrysler '77 and cashed his empty whisky bottles at the vinegar works! McCall liked his Scotch very much and one day, taking off from the Stanley Jones strip he'd had perhaps one nip too many. He flew straight up the Nose Creek Valley and suddenly disappeared over the rim. A fire truck, ambulance and motorcycle went thundering over to see the wreck when he suddenly appeared flying at about 50 feet, and racing above the airstrip, he took the wind sock off the airport tower."

In February 1929 McCall flew one of his most potentially dangerous flights. The railroad and road transportation companies had declined to ship a load of nitroglycerin needed to "shoot" a well at Turner Valley. In his Stinson-Detroiter McCall was to fly from Tulsa, Oklahoma via Great Falls and land at the airstrip on 17th Avenue and 39th Street West in Calgary. A crowd gathered to watch the touchdown and an intrepid newsreel cameraman, secretly hoping to catch shots of the biggest flash fire Calgary had ever seen, braced the tripod of his hand-cranked machine on top of a nearby barn. Jack Peach was there too and said, "We were optimistic despite our bloodthirstiness. We were certain he could fly a garbage can, given sufficient spread to his shirt-tail!"

Soon the plane appeared and the wheels touched down with one bump that sent a horrified gasp up from the crowd and sent them scurrying in all directions. They scarcely dared to look. But there was only silence. They looked up to see that Freddy had set it down gently as a feather, the engine off and the only sound a whirr of the reporter's movie camera. Loaded on a big truck painted with fearsome DANGER warnings the nitro continued on its way to Turner Valley under the care of two white-lipped drivers.

In September 1940 the former war Ace went into uniform again as Flight Lieutenant Fred R. McCall of the Royal Canadian Air Force. He was just as keen as the day he first donned the uniform of the Royal Flying Corps and was anxious to share his experience and incredible flying skill with the thousands of young airmen who would see action overseas.

He returned to Calgary and died here in 1949.

When Calgary's new air terminal was built in 1956, it was named McCall International Airport – a fitting memorial for Fred McCall who was a pioneer as surely as those who came by Red River cart. Only Fred McCall's element was the sky rather than the plains.

✳ ✳ ✳ ✳ ✳

# How the Prince of Wales Got His Ranch

*I*t was at the afternoon tea sponsored by the Association of Southern Alberta Pioneers held at the Calgary Exhibition and Stampede about 1970 that I met Elsie Gordon, daughter of one of the Stampede's founders, George Lane. Lane was born in Des Moines, Iowa, 1856. With a commission and a letter of credit in his pocket, he set out for the foothills of Alberta. In the winter of 1884 Lane was laying the foundation for what would become the greatest cattle business and the most famous cowcamp of the Northwest. He called it the Bar U and the fame of his ranch grew until, as one writer eloquently stated, "A visit to the West without a sojourn at Lane's would be as tame and unprofitable as a trip to Egypt without seeing the pyramids."

Its fame reached the ears of Edward, Prince of Wales who first came to visit in 1919 and was so delighted with the land he decided he wanted a ranch in the area. No one knew better than Elsie how the Prince of Wales got his ranch, which came to be known as the E. P. ranch. Elsie had a personal connection with the piece of land the Prince bought. "It was a piece of the Bedingfield Ranch. Father had made a payment on it for me. I was soon to be married and the land was to be my wedding present. But when the Prince of Wales saw it no other piece of land would satisfy. He had to have it. When he said, 'I want it'– why that was all there was to it, he got it." She paused and then, as though her memory might sound too harsh, she added,

"Well, I guess father felt the community needed help and the Prince would add to the value of their land." George Lane was right about that. Probably nothing in 1929 did more to enhance Alberta's image as a great ranching country than the fact that the Prince of Wales owned a ranch in our foothills.

*Mayor Webster and Edward, Prince of Wales*

\* \* \* \* \*

# Cappy's Smart Reply

My neighbor Dudley Batchelor worked for the City from 1926 to 1963 and told me a funny story about our first fire chief, the redoubtable Cappy Smart.

"Cappy had a thick neck, short and stocky the way you'd expect a navy sub-altern to look and with a loud booming voice that wouldn't require a microphone even if they were invented then. When the Duke of Connaught and his wife visited in 1912 Cappy was invited to show the royal couple the city. The pair was taken to the Palliser penthouse for the marvellous mountain view. The Duchess was talking to Cappy and after admiring the view asked, 'And what were those little brown animals we saw this afternoon?'

'Oh your Highness, those were gophers.'

'What do they do in the winter?' asked the Duchess.

'Oh, they go down in their holes and...' Cappy was stuck for the word *hibernate*. Suddenly he brightened and continued, 'They go down in their holes and fornicate all winter.' His booming voice carried so that everyone in the Royal party heard!

✳ ✳ ✳ ✳ ✳

# Belgian Beauty
# Marie Prince

*1898* – She checked that her gold coins were in the chamois bag and securely fastened to the inside of her chemise; the basket containing what was left of her fruit, meat and vegetables was over her arm. She looked out the window. There was the little station marked Calgary, population 4 000. It had been a long trip. A week on the boat from Liverpool to Montreal, a week more on the boat at Montmorency Falls (near the St. Lawrence) because of navigation difficulties on the St. Lawrence, and yet another week on the stuffy train from Montreal to Calgary – she was looking forward to some clean fresh air. She spoke no English, she was a Belgian. But she was young and beautiful and stepped confidently down onto the station's board platform.

In late 1970 I went to visit Marie, who had been a neighbor of mine in the '50s, to ask her to tell me her life story. She was then 96 years old with an undimmed memory.

She laughed as she remembered stepping down, "The boards were loose. I tripped and fell flat on my face." Fruit, vegetables and her dignity were shattered. At that moment she could have taken the next train back East and never become an important part of the Calgary "story." But Fate had other plans and that very day she met a dashing young man named John Enoch Prince.

John had come from Eau Claire, Wisconsin in 1886 with his father, Peter A. Prince, to make his fortune and was well established as an entrepreneur in Calgary before Marie arrived.

Although Marie spoke no English and John spoke no French, the message must have flashed loud and clear between them. However, Marie wasn't to be rushed into anything and John courted her for six years before he won her. "What were you doing all that time?" I asked.

"What any young girl does," she laughed. "I was going to parties and balls with young men and having a good time. At the time it was reported in *The Herald* that I was *'The most beautiful girl in the most beautiful gown in Calgary!'* at one of the balls, the Hospital Ball, I think. Or it could have been the Firemen's Ball – that was the great social event of the year, staged in the old Hull Opera House on the corner of 6th Avenue and Centre Street. The whole social set of Calgary attended. Everyone was dressed to the gills. I remember one of my gowns – it was blue taffeta with bunches of violets in it and a little drape of chiffon in the front, because it was too *décolleteé* for me." Many of the ladies sent away to the East for their gowns but Marie made and designed her own.

Soon after she arrived in Calgary she worked in Calgary's first dry goods store, Glenville and Robertson's, where she learned both dress-making and millinery skills. Recalling her job at the dry goods store, a wicked twinkle came into her eyes: "I would stay at the ball dancing nearly all the night away. I would get to work on time the next morning all right, but every chance I got throughout the day, I would slip up to the lavatory for a nap."

Not all her work was so selfish. Marie also did hospital work. She helped in the little four-room hospital that once stood where St. Mary's Cathedral now stands. She was a founding member of the ladies' auxiliary to the Holy Cross Hospital, and at 92 years was still doing her stint at wrapping gauze bandages.

The sense of fun and beauty she brought was needed in Calgary in 1898 because day-to-day existence was hard. On the CPR Colonial Special train that brought her to Calgary, Marie had her own mattress and curtains to make her compartment more comfortable and beautiful because it had hard wicker seats in which passengers could only sit bolt-upright. Her coach had a pot-bellied stove where coffee pots warmed all day and on which the "colonials" could cook their own meals – no fancy dining cars for them.

This was only one of the adjustments she had to make. She had come from the comforts of Belgium, New York and Montreal and was a greenhorn aghast when she first sighted her kitchen stove – a big black wood burning monster with six burners and a water tank on the side. Water had to be bought and hauled home in five-gallon jars. The washing machine had to be turned by hand, she had to chop kindling, the list went on and on. "It was work, work, work," Marie remembered.

Her father-in-law Peter Prince was trying to make Calgary life easier with electricity, using a primitive water wheel on the unpredictable Bow River. When the river was low, the electric lights became dim. When there was heavy ice or an ice jam, the big wheel stopped and the town went without lights. The plant, however, was the forerunner of the Calgary Power Company which in 1911 spent a million dollars on a hydro installation at Horse-shoe Falls west of town and provided the power the young city needed for its street cars, homes and industries. The Princes foresaw how Calgary would develop. And of course, they played a large part in its development.

Peter Prince's first enterprise in partnership with I. K. Kerr had been the Eau Claire sawmills built in 1886 on the banks of the Bow, near what is now Centre Street. In its hey-day the mill turned out up to three carloads of lumber a day, and until the 1900s was the chief source of lumber in Calgary and for a radius of 100 miles. They also built the flour mill and original elevator known as the Robin Hood

Mill, and they established the Louis Petrie Wholesale Grocery firm. They organized the John Irwin Grocery Company, were founders of the Calgary Iron Works and the Prince-Kerr Ranch at Brooks.

John Prince was business-minded all the time, recalls Marie. "John postponed our honeymoon to New York 'because of business' he said, but I thought it was a little more than coincidence that when we did go on our trip we just *happened* to go through Chicago where the automobile show just *happened* to be on." John, a car buff, bought one, becoming the owner of the first gas-operated automobile in Calgary.

*Mr. and Mrs. John Prince, c. 1907*

The Princes had their wedding breakfast in the big Prince home, located at what has become the corner of 4th Avenue and 2nd Street S.W. The house is now in Heritage Park. When it was officially welcomed into the park, in 1967, Mrs. Prince was 93 years old. The day of the ceremony, Dave Turner, the park manager, observed she was as perky as a 50 year old, stayed for a couple of sherries and thoroughly enjoyed the whole affair.

The Prince family gave something special to Calgary – fun, beauty, vision, faith in the future. In Marie Prince's words, "I've always loved Calgary. I loved it when I came (my, it was a mess) and I've loved it ever since. I've travelled all over the world and I still like it best. It's just the people . . . the country ."

✳ ✳ ✳ ✳ ✳

# Christmas Treasures

We children felt the usual eager anticipation for Christmas in 1933 – but not our parents. My family had grown to seven children: Joyce, Rob, Ila, Shirley, Ferrol, Laurel and myself. That year the economy was slipping into the dark depths of the Depression. There were so many unemployed men at the Victoria Park community kitchen that they had to be moved to provincial work camps along the Banff highway.

Daddy, too proud to take relief, had finally managed to get a job working for the city doling out payments in the relief department. His pay was extremely low – less than his stipend might have been on relief with seven dependent children. There was hardly enough money for the barest necessities of food and made-over clothes.

This particular Christmas it was Grandmother Casement, who lived on a farm in Southern Alberta, who saved the day. She sent us a few extra dollars, jars of home-canned beef and chicken, crates of eggs, a huge turkey, rich dark Christmas cake and pudding full of fruit and nuts.

What money there was went a long way. I remember my brother Rob bought an appropriate gift for every member of the family for a grand total of two dollars, spats for Daddy for 89 cents and trinkets for Mother and each sister from the Five-and-Ten Cent store.

That Christmas Eve, as Mother and Daddy started to fill our long brown school stockings and lay the gifts around the tree, Mother had that uneasy feeling (known to all mothers of large families at one time or another) that one child did not have as much as the others.

My second sister Ila had desperately wanted a big new doll but it just wasn't her turn for such a costly gift. Mother's heart must have grieved for Ila, so just before she fell exhausted into bed, she slipped a two dollar bill into an envelope with my sister's name on it and propped it up on a branch of the Christmas tree.

The next morning we were so excited we could hardly contain ourselves, but at our house the routine was firmly laid down. It has became a tradition still followed by our own children. We always had to get fully dressed before coming downstairs (none of us knew the luxury of a dressing gown!), eat breakfast and then before going to the tree, line up in order from youngest to eldest. Of course once the line marched toward the tree bedlam broke loose as we were allowed to run and grab presents. We gaily called out each other's names and passed them out to each other.

We opened our stockings with real joy because the Japanese mandarin oranges in the toe were the only fresh fruit we had all winter. From Jenkins Grocerteria chunks of loopy ribbon candy were pepperminty and delicious, as were the hard round candy cylinders imprinted with a delicate rose on top. We would suck and suck, but the rose never vanished until the candy did! Also inside the sock was a handful of nuts. Brazil nuts were an especially rare treat.

As the gaiety and excitement subsided and bits and pieces of tissue paper and red and green string littered the whole living room I, being the eldest, started to pick up the mess. I scooped armfuls of litter and took it out to the unlit burning barrel in the back yard.

Mother, going the rounds to admire what Santa had brought, asked my sister what she was going to buy with her two dollars. "What two dollars?" asked my sister. Nobody had seen it. What a hunt followed!

Although we searched every nook and cranny of the house, looked in and under every present, went through every scrap of paper indoors and out, the two dollars never did show up. But we did not let the loss of the money dampen the Christmas spirit at our house and soon the turkey appeared big and golden, the turnips and potatoes as plentiful as ever and Grandma's pudding delicious as always.

I am glad we didn't long remain sad for the story was to have a very happy ending. The next year, 1934, Mother and Daddy were determined that my sister should have a doll from Santa, and he gave her one. But that wasn't the end of the matter.

You may remember that 1934 was the year when the Dionne quintuplets were born, bringing fame and happy excitement to Canada. Inevitably there were sets of quintuplet dolls ready for sale at Christmas. One set reposed in the window of our neighborhood drug store McGill's. When we walked by, my sisters and I would press our noses against the glass and admire the dolls.

McGill's was offering the dolls as a prize. The store gave points for every purchase made. The customer having the highest total points on Christmas Eve would win the famous dolls.

I suspect that we had been fairly talkative children so that more than one neighbor heard the sad tale of the missing two dollars. Feeling sorry for Ila, some friends must have put her name on their purchases. When the points were totalled my sister had won the quintuplets. She received a total of *six* dolls that Christmas!

✳ ✳ ✳ ✳ ✳

# Mrs. Winter
# – "No nonsense"

*T*he first Ball under the auspices of Cappy Smart and the Calgary Fire Department was held in 1889 in the new firehall. Of the occassion Cappy wrote, "Calgary was continually being referred to by easterners as the centre of the 'wild and wooley west' and this event was intended to show that Calgary possessed as much culture and social refinement as many of the eastern centres." Would Cappy believe we are still struggling to prove that!

One lady that had no problem proving anything to anybody as Mrs. Winter. Mrs. Roland Winter, wife of Judge Winter, was an offhanded, lusty pioneer who launched the Women's Musical Club on its road to success. A large woman, she wore knit skirts almost to her ankles regardless of the prevailing styles, loved large hats tied with a veil over her face and walked with a cane impatiently tapping the floor or sidewalk.

She changed her faith from the Roman Catholic church to marry a Protestant, which took a great deal of courage in those days. She was quite talented – she could write and sing. Her husband played the cello. One day when they were practicing she stopped and glared at him and said bitingly, "You struck the wrong note, you old blighter."

She directed plays at the old Side Door Playhouse. One day as she swept into a rehearsal she was ignored and no one gave her a chair. Not about to let them get away with that nonsense, she marched up to the front of the hall and sat crosslegged on the floor – you can imagine how very shocking that must have been at that time.

For 30 years prior to her death, Mrs. Winter influenced the cultural scene in Calgary. She and Judge Winter lived in a big stone house on the corner of 19th Avenue and 4th Street which was filled with paintings and beautiful *objets d'art* and was the centre of cultural activity for many years until the depression and the death of her husband. No one knows what happened, but at the end she seemed to have only the old house; the artworks were gone. Her daughter was distressed to see her mother as she lay sick and old and asked if she would like to make peace with her church and have a priest call. "Yes, that would be nice," said the old lady.

The priest who came was a novice. As he said the appropriate prayers, Mrs. Winter murmured, "Very nice, very nice." The priest continued. "That was lovely, lovely..." she said. Then her eyes snapped with the liveliness and vigor of earlier days "But your latin is atrocious!" Half an hour later Mrs. Winter died.

*Mrs. Winter*

\* \* \* \* \*

# The C Sharp in Mrs. Sharples

*A*t one of the meetings of the Women's Musical Club in 1912, a number of women were seating themselves in the hall while another group was moving about on the stage. Mrs. Winter, heavily swathed in veils and wearing a coat, looked down from the stage at a timid young woman standing in the doorway and called out in her deep and resonant voice, "Well, who are you?"

"Mrs. Herman Sharples," came the meek reply. None would have guessed that in the years to come this woman would bring the club much of its success and standing in the community. Her lifelong devotion to music began in Victoria, Australia where she was born in 1875. Her musical education began when she was very young and at age 16 she was singing with the comic opera company in Melbourne touring nearly all parts of Australia and New Zealand in first class operas.

It was while working with this company that she met her future husband who was on a business trip from Pennsylvania. After they were married, they embarked on a round-the-world honeymoon. The glamor of the honeymoon dims somewhat for me when I discovered Mrs. Sharples was soon pregnant and gave birth to a son at the end of the trip, which had included many delays at terminal stations and rough sea voyages. However, their globe-trotting had taken them through Calgary, the city to which they were to return and spend the rest of their lives. Both became active in musical circles and much credit must also go to Mr. Sharples, who entertained at their home visiting celebrities such as Jascha Heifitz, Fritz Kreisle, Rachmaninoff, Galli-Curci, John McCormick and Sir Ernest Macmillan.

Typical of the enthusiasm of "musical" ladies in those days, the Women's Musical Club prevailed upon the Duke of Connaught to present certificates of merit to the students of the Royal Academy of Music while he was here for the first Calgary Stampede. Mrs. Sharples was busy with activities in the Women's Musical Club and the Apollo Choir when World War I began and her son enlisted and went overseas. During her first term as president of the Musical Club, while preparing to chair the afternoon meeting, she received a telegram announcing the death of her only son. This courageous woman not only insisted that the meeting continue, but that she would announce the musical numbers. Left with no children of her own, Mrs. Sharples threw herself into helping other children. She was inspired to begin Local Composers' Day which gave an audience for beginners starting out on musical careers. One of the first on the young composers' platform was five year old Minuetta Schumiatcher, who presented her own compositions. Minuetta went on to fame as a pianist and composer in the United States and held Composers' Days for her own students in Boston.

Mrs. Sharples also worked tirelessly for the Red Cross and during the two World Wars established records for knitting socks and sweaters; from October 1939 to the end of 1941, she had knit 245 articles! She was also president of the Mothers and Widows of War Association.

Mrs. Sharples was resident secretary of the Royal Schools of Music of London for 28 years. Calgary was well known because of Mrs. Sharples, many scholarship winners (such as Gladys Egbert). Therefore examiners came here to conduct examinations. Small wonder, after such distinguished service to the community, that in 1955 Mrs. Sharples won Calgary's Distinguished Citizen's Award.

✳ ✳ ✳ ✳ ✳

# *A Riverside Family*

When I was in Grade 8 at Earl Grey Elementary school it was for the most part attended by the descendants of Anglo-Saxon pioneers. We had inter-city basketball games and whenever the teams from Riverside School were coming we were apprehensive and extra determined to win. They were tough competitors and many spoke with a slight accent. It was unfortunate that not one of our teachers thought to tell us the history of the students and their families at Riverside. When I interviewed John George Morasch and his younger sister Katherina Leinweber I learned a bit of of it. John was 101 years old at the time, sitting in his armchair with his hands resting on top of his cane.

Their family story goes back to 1763 when Catherine II, Czarina of Russia, born a German princess, issued a manifesto which was one of the most enticing land settlement schemes ever devised, supassing even Canada's CPR land promotions. It included the right to self-government, religious liberty, exemption from military service forever, a grant of land to every family, their own churches, schools and free transportation. Catherine's invitation revived the hopes and dreams of Germans suffering from the ruin and devastation of the Seven Year's War. Many, especially farmers, joined in the trek which took them on 2 000 mile journey into the vastness of Russia. They suffered freezing cold, snow and attacks by wolves until they reached an unusually beautiful area on the Volga River. However there were no homes, only a few plows and sickles. The community held on to their German nationality, customs and language and with great toil and effort produced wheat, oats, rye, barley, cucumbers, apple orchards, cherry trees and many strawberries. "Our town name Jagodnaja meant 'strawberry' in Russian," laughed Mr. Morasch.

Crops were abundant but threshing was primitive and became a family affair. The event was like an extended camping trip as they packed special trunks for food and barrels for water. Everyone went to work in the fields outside of town. Meat was provided by butchering their own livestock and pork sausage was a specialty. According to Russian custom sunflower oil was used extensively in their cooking. After the harvest, it was time for dancing and weddings. "The older ladies cooked the wedding suppers," said Katherina, "barley soup, roast beef and potatoes...."

"With lots of krebbles!" interrupted John. A krebble is like a donut made of bread dough, rolled out and cut in strips with two slits in it so you can twist it into a bow, then deep fried and served with sour cream – very rich and very delicious.

John Morasch was born in 1876 and up to that time the community of German Russians had been progressing so well that certain Russian circles, out of jealousy or fear, slowly succeeded in eroding their religious freedom and the military exemption. In addition, the amount of land apportioned was reduced so that John's generation grew up with a passion to own more land. Consequently, when advertisements somehow reached them, telling of the great opportunities in Alberta, John Morasch, his two brothers and sister left for Canada.

"Seven days out at sea an officer came and asked where we were going," said John. "Calgary, Canada, we answered. Mumbling something about not being eligible for Canada because of 'eye' infections the officer replied, 'Now I tell you the truth, you are going to South America.'" This tactic was often used as a clever ploy to fill different ship quotas. John continued, "Men who had been big shots back home were told to 'do this' and 'do that' with a pick and shovel. I can remember sitting behind a rock and crying when I thought of the good land we'd left."

After four years of menial work he and one of his brothers made their way up to Calgary in 1911. John soon became a foreman for the CPR caboose painters. Realizing that this city was the longed-for land of opportunity he wrote letters persuading the rest of the family to come in 1913. A Lutheran church, always the centre of their lives, had already been built in Calgary by men like Henry and Conrad Kromm, John Schneidmiller and John Luft.

As in Russia, families did not easily mix with people of different backgrounds but clung together in the Calgary community known as Riverside. Money was scarce but, as granddaughter Elsie Krom remembered, "It didn't seem that bad to us as children. We had no store bought toys but we always had a wagon for summer and a sleigh for winter and amused ourselves with games like hopscotch, jump-the-rope, marbles, see-saw and ball games outside in summertime and games like Parcheesie, Flinch and Dominoes indoors in wintertime (playing by the light of oil lamps)." When the other kids started calling them names about being German at the beginning of the First World War they just settled the whole thing with a tug-of-war. Unfortunately some adults were not that sensible.

By 1916, when the war had dragged on for over two years, feeling ran high against the Kaiser and all Germans. Sparked by a rumor that the owner of the White Lunch Café had fired an ex-soldier and hired a German, a group of drunk soldiers and civilians set off an anti-German riot. They wrecked the café and the Riverside Hotel.

"I was there when that hotel was built," said Katherina, "and I couldn't believe my eyes when I saw them take anything they could and break it – they even heaved a piano out the second floor window! They yelled, 'We'll kill those bloody Germans!' We grabbed forks, clubs, anything to protect ourselves. We were afraid to go out on the streets for awhile."

Afterwards Mayor Costello called a special meeting of Calgary City Council and enlisted the aid of officers in charge at Sarcee Military Camp to keep their men under control and on base until tensions eased. Despite such measures Katherina continued, "My husband was fired from his job with the CPR so we went to the United States for six months until Calgarians realized none of us had ever lived in Germany." There was no bitterness in her words for she realized that few Calgarians outside their own Riverside community ever understood the enigma of third generation Russians who spoke German, but felt allegiance to no country but Canada.

✳ ✳ ✳ ✳ ✳

# "Calamity Nell"

*N*ellie McClung's house is located at 803 - 15th Avenue S.W. What a lovely old house it is! Some years ago I was delighted when I drove up one crisp winter day to see the distinguished looking two-storey Tudor house with the clapboards painted a warm dark brown, the windows and roof a snappy bright red, and a picket fence surrounding the spacious lawns.

At the door I was met by Mrs. Bessie Smith. She welcomed me into a spacious entrance graced with a curving staircase and an oak newal post complete with a bronze statuette. My eyes swept along the polished floors into the living room dominated by a large brick open fireplace before which chesterfields were placed to enjoy the blaze.

"This part of the house is almost exactly as Nellie McClung left it," she said. My heart beat faster as I realized I was standing exactly where my mother stood 50 years earlier being welcomed by Nellie herself to a Wesley United Church Good Cheer Club tea.

As we settled in front of the fire with cookies and tea, Mrs. Smith brought out a scrapbook of clippings on the life of Nellie McClung. It was then I realized that this house still stood only because Bessie Smith's admiration for Nellie had inspired her to refuse high offers from developers and made her determined to wait for some government to move to preserve it.

For those of you who might not know, Nellie McClung bequeathed to every woman in Canada a most priceless heritage – the right to vote, and recognition as a "person" in the laws of Canada. It is a measure of her popularity that at least five Canadian cities claim Nellie as their own and that a commemorative stamp was issued on the 100th anniversary of her birth.

Yet millions of Canadians have never heard of her. A vigorous advocate of social reform and women's suffrage, Nellie McClung attained position and honors in public life unmatched by any Canadian woman of the time.

Her support of the war effort was rewarded by an appointment to the Canadian War Conference in 1918. In 1921 she was the first Canadian woman-delegate to attend an international ecumenical conference of the Methodist Church. That same year she was elected to the Alberta legislature, where she remained as a member for Edmonton until 1926. From 1936 to 1942 she served as the first woman member of the Canadian Broadcasting Corporation's Board of Governors. She also served as a Canadian delegate to the League of Nations in 1938.

Such an inventory of her achievements leaves one breathless; but how did Nellie McClung start out?

It would seem most likely to assume such genius sprouted from a home of social privilege and education, but Nellie was born in 1873 of a moderately-educated, hard-working family. Her father, John Mooney, was one of the farmers forced out of Ireland by the potato famine, and her mother, Letitia McCurdy, was a strict puritanical Scotswoman from Dundee.

Nellie was the youngest of their six children born on a Chatsworth, Ontario farm where Nellie wrote "the stones lay on the fields like flocks of sheep."

When she was six the family left Chatsworth and travelled by stage to Owen Sound, by boat to Duluth, by train to St. Boniface and finally, by ox cart over the sparsely inhabited prairie to arrive at Milford, Manitoba. A log cabin, unchinked, with one window in the west end, a hay-thatched roof and a rough board floor awaited them as their new homestead.

Nellie grew to her middle teens on this farm. Her only grievances then were going barefoot in the cold to bring in the cows for milking and as the youngest, almost never getting any new clothes.

Although she couldn't read a word when she started school at the age of ten, she graduated from Winnipeg's Normal School with a teacher's certificate when she was 16. After two years of teaching, she took six months of Collegiate which completed her formal education.

It wasn't formal schooling that led Nellie McClung to her political heights, rather, it was her determination to relieve the prairie women she saw living a dead existence in shacks with nothing – none of the modern amenities, no electricity, refrigerators, telephones, radios, newspapers or cars. And for many it was a new baby every year.

She wrote of one woman who was taken to a mental hospital. When the doctor questioned her husband on the cause of her lapse from reason, he answered "It beats me where she could've got it, she hasn't been off the farm for six years."

Nellie's enthusiastic devotion and zeal would carry her causes far. But it was her secret weapon – her priceless gift of a sense of humor that spread her message far and wide. She had it in all her writings and in her lectures. No matter how serious the subject, there were always chuckles and laughter. She saw humor in other people and best of all, she could laugh at herself.

Nellie told this joke on herself. She was in favor of the prohibition of alcohol. While teaching at Somerville she thought she would demonstrate to the class the evil of drink, so she put two glasses on the desk and into each dropped a worm. The one in the water was quite lively but the one dropped into the glass of whisky died. She turned to the class and asked, "What lesson do we learn from this?", and one little boy put up his hand, "Yes, Johnny?"

"We learn that if we have lots of whisky, we'll never have worms."

It was while at this school that Nellie came under two influences which changed the course of her life. One was the writer Charles Dickens, who showed that mountains of injustice in social order could be changed by writing. The other was the wife of the new Methodist clergyman from the East, Mrs. McClung, who taught the Sunday School class Nellie attended. Mrs. McClung taught Nellie strong Methodist Church values and practices. Nellie must be the only woman in history to have fallen in love with her mother-in-law before she met her husband!

Mrs. McClung's son Wes had remained back East to complete his courses in pharmacy. But he returned to his family and became the clerk in the local drug store. Not long after Nellie walked the three miles to the village with all the money she had ($3) and, according to Pansy Pue (former Calgary alderman) who knew Nellie well, "She spent it all on a fountain pen and kept the clerk occupied for as long as she could showing her how the pen worked. From that day on Wes never had a chance!"

As soon as Wes took over the drug business in Manitou they were married and moved into the four small rooms above the store. Starting out they had $4 in cash between the two of them. They planned to have a family of six, but settled for five. All the children were born very closely together.

Through it all, Nellie fretted about writing. Even with the help of faithful Alice, the housekeeper who stayed with her for 17 years, there was never enough time to write.

One morning, when the fourth baby was just a few weeks old, her mother-in-law came bringing news of a short-story contest for new writers. She urged Nellie, "Drop everything right now, and get at it. Alice and I will take care of things." By night, Nellie had written the first chapter of *Sowing Seeds in Danny*. It was eventually accepted by a publisher who urged her to develop it into the book which became a Canadian best-seller. This launched her career as a writer. She produced 16 books (most were written when she was in Alberta) and collections of short stories which appeared in a syndicated newspaper column.

After 15 successful years with the drug store, Wes sold out and joined a life insurance company which moved them to Winnipeg. There, Nellie locked political horns with pompous Premier Sir Rodmond Roblin, who had utter contempt for the idea that women should vote. He "didn't know why women needed to ferret out disgusting things, like women working in cold, airless factories without separate toilets."

In this case Nellie's gift of humor succeeded where the efforts of countless suffragettes had failed. She and her friends formed the Political Equality League which scheduled a well-advertised "women's parliament." At the event Nellie, with her wonderful powers of mimicry, parroted Sir Rodmond's every inflection, gesture and pose and supplied a few choice arguments of her own as to why men were not competent to govern the country, and therefore could not be trusted with the vote.

The League's aim was to make the government attitude to women appear ridiculous and they succeeded. It became a riot of fun for the audience and the press loved it. The women gave one repeat performance and it is believed that this burlesque, more than anything else, brought the vote to women in Manitoba in 1916. Alberta and Saskatchewan followed that same year.

The publicity was good for her cause and made Nellie much in demand as a lecturer. It also made her many enemies – she was nicknamed "Calamity Nell," and was even hung in effigy. But she carried on, undaunted and supported by her husband. With an attitude few men could manage to muster even today, Wes would laugh and say, "Just call me Mr. Nellie McClung, I don't mind."

Of her five children Nellie once said, "they make me vulnerable in five places," and she was often criticized for being away from home and the children.

Mrs. Pippard (of Calgary) travelled with Nellie on her "prohibition tours" and remembered a meeting in the Town Hall at High River, where cowboys in the balcony sat insolently with their spurred boots up on the polished rail. Nellie came out on the stage with her hands on her hips, her head held high, one foot firmly planted forward and stared then down. One by one the boots returned to the floor. "Why don't you go home and look after your own children?"someone growled.

"My children are bathed and fed, and safely at home with their father," she smiled, "so you need have no worries about them."

*Nellie McClung, a.k.a. Calamity Nell*

The family moved again, from Winnipeg to Edmonton. There Nellie was elected Liberal member of the Alberta legislature when the United Farmers swept to power in 1921.

It did not bother Nellie at all to cut across party lines and join hands with opposition cabinet minister Irene

Parlby on many issues of social legislation. Even though the two ladies succeeded in getting hot lunches and medical care for school children and a municipal hospital, Nellie was disappointed that her pleas for temperance legislation were ignored.

It was while in Edmonton that she made the friends who were to form the powerful alliance which upset the Supreme Court of Canada's ruling of 1879, "*That women are persons in matter of pains and penalties, but are not persons in matters of rights and privileges.*"

In 1929 the women learned that an appeal against that Supreme Court ruling could be filed by any five persons. Nellie, Irene Parlby, Magistrate Emily Murphy (first woman magistrate in the British Empire), Louise McKinney of Claresholm (also an ex-member of the Alberta legislature) and Mrs. Henrietta Edwards of Macleod (who had written a book entitled *Laws Affecting Women*) joined in an appeal to the federal government in Ottawa. It was denied.

Their last hope was the Privy Council of England, and when their petition was received and that body ruled that women were indeed persons, the last barrier to women's participation in public life was removed.

There was a victory celebration held in Calgary's Palliser Hotel which Pansy Pue attended. "The place was jammed. I have never been among a more excited or enthusiastic crowd. "The Five Famous Women," as they were nicknamed, were all there and each spoke briefly. Their hearts were full and their faces glowed with happiness. They believed 'the brave new world' had arrived."

That was in 1929. But the battle was far from over. "Now that we've been admitted to the Senate, there are only two great institutions which don't accept women on equal terms," Nellie said, "the church and the beer parlors."

Nellie participated in a small victory where the church was concerned. She packed folks into Central United Church to support Lydia Gruch who travelled from town to town by horse and buggy to preach. She was not allowed to practice the sacraments or perform marriages, despite the fact she achieved the highest marks in her graduating class in theology at St. Andrews College, Saskatoon. It was thirteen years before the men of the United Church allowed Lydia Gruch's ordination.

Of beer parlors Nellie said, "We think women ought to be let in. Not that we wouldn't be better out than in, but we believe in equality." But she had less success in this area.

The growing Depression focused Nellie's concern on the poor. With no government social services available, her Wesley United Church Good Cheer Club helped fill part of the gap in Calgary. "It feeds, clothes, guides, cheers and strengthens, and all the time the girls themselves have a good time," she wrote. Even after her retirement to Victoria in 1934, Nellie wrote letters to Louise Dean, life member of the group, describing money-raising schemes they could use.

In 1933 the Oxford Movement burst upon the world scene, and Nellie embraced it in a desperate hope that it was a solution to world problems. "Before long," recalled Louise Dean, "Mrs. McClung realized that the public recitation of so-called 'sins,' one of the basic tenets of the Movement, while having a salutary effect on the confessor, was not helping the country's poor." Honors and broad avenues of service at the national and international level crowded upon Nellie, but she always had time for one thing more in Calgary.

She helped to found the Calgary branch of the Canadian Federation of Business and Professional Women with Pansy Pue and other "like-minded" women. This was the group which later installed a bronze plaque at the entrance to the Senate chambers honoring the Five Famous Women. "Women's groups across Canada offered contributions but the five were all Albertans and Alberta women felt that it was their duty and privilege to pay for it," said Pansy Pue with pride.

*Tablet commemorating victory of the Famous Five, 1938*

*Prime Minister Mackenzie King (centre), Nellie McClung (far right)*

Many idealists are too busy to practice what they preach, but young girls and women in trouble came to Nellie McClung for advice and none were every turned away unhelped or uncomforted. She always engaged "Old Country" girls for help in her home but, while some house-wives treated these girls little better than chattels, Nellie taught each girl to read and speak English and they were given a regular evening when they could invite friends to the house and entertain them in the living room. Three of her "girls" were married from her home.

Nellie's ghost may well be hovering over that Calgary home now that it has been declared a historic site. Those of us who worked to save her home hope that some day it will be used in a manner which makes a fitting memorial to her vision of a better world for women. Nellie McClung would appreciate that.

\* \* \* \* \*

# The Family of Man

*R*obert M. Cummings of Montreal was one of the "Sons" of Maxwell Cummings & Sons, a large Canadian development company. He was compelled to spend a great deal of time in Calgary during 1966 and 1967, constructing the imposing Calgary Place complex, the Pacific Petroleum Building and others. As he and my husband, Mayor Jack Leslie, stood admiring the Armengol statues at Montreal's Expo '67, Mr. Cummings said, "In some cities developers are intimidated by individuals at City Hall expecting pay-offs 'under the table' but I've found none of that in Calgary. I've had great co-operation from everyone from you to the construction crews. I think I'd like to make a gift to Calgary."

At a cost of around $150 000 he purchased the Armengol Sculptures (specifically commissioned for part of Britain's Pavilion at Expo) at the conclusion of the Expo and paid an additional $75 000 to have them transported to Calgary. They now stand in front of the Calgary Education Centre. We call them the Family of Man and they have become the most photographed "family" in Calgary. Standing 21 feet tall yet unmistakably human – naked, raceless, expressionless, they extend hands in gestures of fellowship and goodwill. These sculptures were conceived and designed by Mario Armengol who aimed to inspire two moods – an immediate reaction of insignificance and dependence. No wonder then, they have been cursed as being ungainly, even unGodly, yet also praised as a magnificent contribution to the city's cultural scene.

*Unveiling of the Armengol statues in Calgary, 1968*

I was there that sunny day in July, 1968 when workmen were hauling away scaffolding and laying the last strips of sod around the feet of the statues, minutes before their Royal Highnesses the Duke and Duchess of Kent arrived to dedicate and accept the statues on behalf of the City of Calgary. Somehow the circle seemed complete. From Britain to Montreal...given by a Montrealer to Calgary...dedicated by a member of the British Royal Family. I feel the Armengol Sculptures are one of Calgary's most outstanding city attractions and I am grateful for their presence. To me they are a tangible token of thanks to Calgarians.

\* \* \* \* \*

# Last of the Covered Wagon Pioneers

"The 24th of May is the Queen's birthday – if you don't give us a holiday we'll all run away." My sister Joyce and I happily chanted the ditty as we bounced along beside Daddy. I was just ten and he was taking us on our once-a-year adventure into Chinatown to buy firecrackers for the occassion. We walked, of course. Who had a car in 1930? It was not too far for we lived on 7th Avenue West, right where Elveden house stands today. Now one of Calgary's busiest downtown thoroughfares, then it was a lovely residential street where tall leafy poplars met in an arch over the roadway. Chinatown was on Centre Street. The shops were below street level so we had to go down steps to get into the stores. What delightful spine-tingling apprehension was created in our young minds by our sur-roundings. Strange-looking meats hung in greasy windows and bizarre inked characters (Chinese writing) displayed over the vegetable stands. A proprietor shuffled behind his counter, speaking very little English and only a burlap curtain hung between the store and who knew what mysteries in the back.

All this was many years before a man named Mew Chuck Wing came to call every week at my family home in South Calgary with fresh fruits and vegetables to sell. We knew him simply as John Mew. He was born in Canton, China but would never tell his age – we guessed he was born around 1890. He came to Calgary in 1911 when there were 482 Chinese men in the city, but only three women. Like many other Chinese men, John had hoped to make enough money to send soon for his wife but the Canadian government's discouraging "head tax" on Chinese women then stood at $500 which seemed to him (and many others) an impossible sum to save. Then on July 1, 1923 an Act called the Chinese Immigration Act forbade the entrance of Chinese women altogether. We might celebrate July 1st as a national holiday but many Chinese families then looked on it as a day of mourning for their lost rights and loved ones far away.

John Mew first came by in a wagon covered with canvas with a little coal-burning stove in back during winter to keep the produce from freezing. A tired looking horse pulled it all winter and summer. Other wagons came in those days, with bread, milk and ice, but his outfit intrigued my sisters and I more for it suggested to us the pioneers who came from eastern Canada so many years before with all their worldly goods in wagons covered with canvas. By the 1960s John's wagon had long been replaced by a green panel truck.

For 50 years John sent money back to his family in China. His wife arrived to be with him for only the last few years of his life. He brought her to meet my mother on one occassion but most days he would ask to borrow the phone to call her and seemed to delight in saying her name, "Hello Mrs. Mew. How are you Mrs. Mew?"

Through the years John had made a host of friends, among them the customers on his route all over South Calgary. He invited my mother and some of the neighbors down to his home for a wonderful dinner one evening before his wife arrived in Canada. The guests reported, "You could have eaten off the floor it was so clean." What a revelation that would have been to some prominent Calgary citizens like James Short, who in 1910 petitioned City Council, protesting the construction of Chinatown on the grounds that "they (the Chinese) have not the first idea of cleanliness or sanitation." Fortunately other Calgarians, like our friend William Porterfield, defended the Chinese and the petition failed.

John was interested in what went on in the city. In politics, he did more than many citizens in campaigning for his favorite candidates. John was also interested in all the pregnancies on his route and rejoiced, especially when the new baby was a boy. Then he had a gift such as a stuffed feathered parrot on a ring for the baby, and for the mother a pretty box full of fresh ginger. His honesty was beyond question bordering almost on the self righteousness. On one occassion he spied a set of scales in one customer's kitchen and thereafter he refused to serve her again. No amount of explaining that the scales had been used to weigh some meat, not his produce, would make him relent. But he had a generous soul. After my father lost his sight John brought the best grapes, the firmest bananas, the biggest and freshest strawberries all at special low prices. He even visited Daddy in the Colonel Belcher Hospital where he took large baskets of fruit for my father because he was not just his customer, but his friend.

Mew Chuck Wing died in Calgary in August, 1970. When they opened the casket at his funeral there, lying on his breast, was the old fedora hat he had worn on his deliveries. And as the mourners left the little Chinese United Church in old Chinatown each person received, in a handmade manila envelope, one bittersweet candy and five cents – John's last bequest to his friends.

✳ ✳ ✳ ✳ ✳

# Mr. Bennett Goes to Ottawa

*T*he Right Honorable Richard Bedford Bennett had no trouble becoming the hero of my Grade V class of McDougall School in 1931, for he was the donor and we the happy recipients of the coveted R. B. Bennett Shield and Medal for Best Physical Training Junior Girls at Calgary Public Schools. Although he was the unable to present the trophy he sent a bowler-hatted executive assistant and we were all very impressed.

A few weeks later, after much serious thought, I announced to my mother that I knew what I wanted to be when I grew up – R. B. Bennett's secretary.

It was hard for me to understand why he became so hated by some. I began to understand why after I talked to an old southern Saskatchewan farmer who, 40 years later said with bitterness, "Sure he paid a bonus of 5 cents a bushel in 1931 but we didn't have any wheat! The farmers in the north of the province that had wheat to sell got a bonus. Everything in the south was dried out so we got nothing." Unfortunately the Saskatchewan farmers with wheat believed that the Winnipeg Grain Exchange was forcing down the price of wheat when they bought from farmers in order to inflate the price at which it was sold to the consumer. Although Bennett set up a Royal Commission to investigate their Wheat Board, and by 1935 his policy paid off for farmers, they continued to think of him as a man unmoved by the poverty and desperation of his fellow Canadians.

Yet to those few who knew him intimately he was a sentimental man, easily moved to tears. I interviewed J. J. Saucier Q. C., prominent Calgary lawyer and at one time Bennett's executive assistant in Ottawa, and Pansy Pue, former Calgary alderman and fiesty Conservative Party worker, told me that Bennett "gave money away, literally by the handful."

"Bags of mail from supplicants came in every day that he was in Parliament. He had two senior female secretaries who had power of attorney on his bank account and they used to enclose $5 or $10 in return letters. They could imitate his signature extremely well and would be in there typing all day, acknowledging receipt of the appeals and replying, *'I'm sorry I can't send more but I am enclosing $10....'* "I wonder where those people were when the hurtful stories of "iron-heel" Bennett were going around.

∗  ∗  ∗

R. B. Bennett was born in 1870 at Hopewell Cape in the province of New Brunswick. He came to Calgary in 1897 with a ton of books in his trunks and $100 in his pocket. He registered at the old Alberta Hotel which boasted of its bar as the longest between Winnipeg and Vancouver. This hardly impressed R. B. On his first day in Calgary a hospitable Calgarian invited him into the bar for a drink and he said, "No thank you, I don't drink." Another offered him a cigar and he said, "No thank you, I don't smoke."

"You don't drink and you don't smoke! Hell," said the Calgarian, "you won't last long around here!"

A young man of 27, he had exchanged the certainties of his New Brunswick life and law practice for the vagaries of a life in the almost new city of Calgary in the Northwest Territories. He came as a law partner with Senator J. A. Lougheed. That Bennett, bereft of any outward show of warmth, ever got anywhere in politics in the first place is to me rather remarkable, for, as CPR solicitor he had to defend that "hated giant" against down-to-earth persons like Mother Fulham. She was Calgary's Irish "pig woman," whose cow was killed by a CPR train in spite of signs forbidding entrance to the right-of-way. Her priceless remark "And what makes ye think me poor old cow could read?" made the CPR, and Bennett, look hardhearted and foolish. And, of course, public sympathy went to Bob Edwards when he, thanks to Bennett, lost his CPR pass for scathing anti-CPR editorials and cartoons in his Calgary Eye Opener. Yet how many would know that Bennett paid Edwards' funeral expenses?

Nevertheless, in 1898 Bennett won his first seat in the Territorial Assembly and in 1909 was returned a member for Calgary in the Alberta Legislature. He led our city in early negotiations with our rival community Edmonton, when each was determined to be the capital of the province. R. B. always claimed that the Liberal administration welshed on a gentleman's agreement under which Edmonton would be the capital and Calgary would have the university. We got neither.

In 1911, he was successful in his first venture into national politics and took a place in Sir Robert Borden's government. He chose not to run in 1917, but was persuaded by Arthur Meighen to stand for election in 1921. In what Mr. Saucier described as "the fountain pen election," Bennett was in great demand as a speaker and being perhaps a little overconfident of his own Calgary South seat he spent a good deal of time speaking across Canada. In spite of that, when the ballots were counted he had a majority until it was revealed that, for reasons no one now knows, a considerable number of his supporters marked their ballots with fountain pens instead of the pencil provided in the polling booths. It was ruled and upheld in all the courts that those ballots were spoiled and invalid and R. B. Bennett lost the seat by 16 votes.

He used the years out of politics to practice law vigorously and was very active in business, becoming director of an imposing number of large corporations like Metropolitan Life, Imperial Oil, the Royal Bank and the E. B. Eddy Company. This is when he made his money, not, as later stories had it, "at the expense of the rest of the people" when he was in political office. He was a tremendous advocate, doing things in court most lawyers wouldn't dare do. "For example," said Saucier, "if all else failed, he'd pick a quarrel with the judge making him so wrathful that he'd foul things up so there would have to be a new trial before a different judge." Clients loved it.

He was a one-man legal aid system before anybody ever invented the expression. If someone with modest means came along who had some kind of legal problem or was in trouble, he would not only provide his services free of charge but would spend great sums of his own money and fight the case to the "foot of the throne" – one of his expressions for the Privy Council in London. To do this he had to run back and forth by trans-Atlantic steamer and he was a very poor sailor. Mr. Saucier remembers crossing with him one summer. "He was all right as long as he stayed put. On the voyage he stayed in bed all the time. My job was to keep him supplied with enough "Whodunits."

In 1927 Bennett won the leadership of the Conservative Party, withdrew completely from law practice, resigned all his directorships and moved to Ottawa to devote himself fully to leading the party into its 1930 victory. He always drew a full house in Parliament. He had a magnificent voice – pleasant but powerful and he had a tremendous command of the English language which he attributed to reading the King James version of the Bible.

Devoted to his mother, who was a deeply religious Methodist, he read a certain number of verses of the Bible every day and knew much of it by heart. He used Biblical quotations in debate most effectively and held everyone's attention. R. B. had a phenomenal memory and a very quick mind, remembering things his opponents had done 25 years earlier.

But there is more to politics than oratory and one of his great weaknesses was that he tried to do far too much himself. "When the House was in session the hours were dreadful – nine in the morning till the middle of the next night. I was young but I'd get to the stage where I was walking around in a daze. Not Bennett – he was always alert and when everything else was done he'd catch up on his letters with two secretaries sitting opposite him in the prime minister's office in the east block. He would give one a rapid burst and while she was catching up, give the other a rapid burst. It was astounding the amount of dictation he could do," remembered Mr. Saucier.

*R.B. Bennett*

Although he encouraged physical fitness by donating trophies such as the one my class won, by giving money to junior football teams, and sending Captain Alex Ferguson's schoolboy cadets to compete in England, Bennett himself did not participate in any sports activities. Instead he indulged himself in boxes of divinity fudge from lady supporters. The only thing that prevented his health from cracking up sooner than it did was that he always observed the Sabbath Day. At midnight on Saturday he stopped work and didn't resume until midnight on Sunday. He had those 24 hours off when he'd relax, read and go to church.

Recalled Miss Ruth Patterson (a secretary of the Bennett law firm for over fifty years and also a member of the choir at Central United Church), "Mr. Bennett counted the number in attendance in the choir at church and next morning a cheque for the amount of $1 would arrive at the church office for each member that was present. Typical of his thoughtfulness, he also provided the padded seats in the choir loft."

According to Mr. Saucier, Bennett was the last hard-money prime minister and moved heaven and earth to defend the dollar. "He regarded inflation as legalized robbery of pensioners. He probably took a rather extreme view but most people are only now beginning to appreciate what a dreadful thing inflation is, the suffering it causes and the general upheaval of the whole economy that it creates."

One of his most outstanding accomplishments was the Imperial Conference of 1932, and the Imperial Preferences that endured until the United Kingdom entered the Common Market, which were undoubtedly of tremendous benefit economically to Canada. No, Bennett did not defeat the Depression – but neither did any other world leader. I was among those who grew up believing that he lost the election of 1935 because he was too "conservative" and wouldn't support reform, but study of his speeches of that campaign reveal just the opposite. Bennett said, " If you believe that in capitalism there are abuses which work hardship upon the people of this country, if you believe that the faults of capitalism have brought about injustices in our social state, if you believe that these injustices manifest themselves in lower wages and too high cost of living and unemployment – then support my party...the worker, when unemployed, must, with the help of the state, be provided with the means to effect his own security against unemployment. This security will be provided by means of unemployment insurance."

To me he sounded more like Woodsworth and the CCF. It appears that Bennett was so far ahead of others in his own party that they became confused and failed to follow. But one cannot fault his foresight that these reforms would come. Nor can one fault his major accomplishments – the St. Lawrence Waterway Treaty, initiating the CBC, setting up the Bank of Canada, guiding the Prairie Farm Rehabilitation Act through Parliament.

Every year, from 1922 to the present, the top two boys and girls in Grades 9 and 12 in Calgary have been the recipients of an R. B. Bennett (later Viscount Bennett) Scholarship. His concern for Calgary's young people carries on to this day and they, as well as the rest of us should remember and admire R. B. Bennett as a politician of absolute integrity who used his whole energy and his considerable personal fortune to forward the party he believed in. He was the kind of person that makes our democratic party system work. R. B. Bennett should have a prominent place in Calgary's history. After all, how many prime ministers have we sent to Ottawa in our 100 years? None but Richard Bedford Bennett.

\* \* \* \* \*

# The Shortest Time in Parliament

Colonel D.G.L. Cunnington (OBE, MC, VD, ED, CD) claimed to have the shortest parliamentary stay on record.

In 1940 Colonel Cunnington was an "old soldier" whose life was already a legend – he rose from private to colonel in less than three years. While in France he was left for dead on a battlefield, but he returned home two months after his supposedly "widowed" wife had cashed in his insurance policy and begun to collect a pension. When I met him he was 88 and he vigourously prowled around his small Roxboro living room (he couldn't talk to anyone sitting down) telling me of his foray into politics.

"The by-election was called in September 1939 after R. B. Bennett had resigned his Calgary seat in January of that year. The nomination meeting was held in the old Central Park Library. When I walked in I thought I was "sunk" when I saw the big crowd and my two powerful opponents (both prominent Calgarians) Dr. W. A. Lincoln and Fred Shouldice. But things took a surprising turn when Shouldice withdrew. A. L. Smith, who proposed me, gave one of his gung-ho speeches – and I won."

"Then there I was, all prepared to fight to keep the old Bennett seat for the Conservatives when the liberal candidate Manley Edwards withdrew. So I won by acclamation – what a heady victory!"

"The House of Parliament was to convene on January 25, 1940. On that day, after the opening ceremonies and the Speech from the Throne, the Commons trouped back from the Senate and took their places. The new members (including me) were called in and introduced. The introduction, if you've never seen it, is quite a performance. The Speaker announced my name and consituency and I entered and took a few steps toward the Speaker and bowed and then proceeded from the rear of the Chamber to the foot of the Table, bowed again. My escort then said 'Mr. Speaker, I have the honor to present to you Colonel D.G.L. Cunnington, member for Calgary West who has taken the Oath, signed the Roll and now claims the right to take his seat.'

The Speaker said, 'Let the honorable Member take his seat.' I stepped down, bowed yet again and departed by the rear of the Speaker's chair (as I had been carefully instructed) and took my seat. Then Prime Minister Mac-Kenzie King made a speech. Dr. Manion (a new member like myself) made one also and after that they passed a bill of some kind to show that the House was officially in session. Then we adjourned for lunch. While we were at lunch in the Commons restaurant we heard that King, anxious to get a war mandate, got in touch with the Govenor General who promptly dissolved the House. We never even went back in to the afternoon sitting. I had sat in the House for just three hours!"

Colonel Cunnington lost out to Liberal Manley Edwards in his second political campaign but he continued to give his tremendous energy and zeal to the community and the armed forces. He was a founding father of the Alberta United Services Institute, he organized and commanded the Calgary Tank Regiment (now the King's Own Calgary Regiment), commanded the 24th Infantry Brigade and organized the 19th Field Brigade RCA, becoming its commanding officer and later its honorary Colonel.

The dubious honor of sitting the shortest time in parliament was a blow at first, but it didn't slow the Colonel down for long.

✳ ✳ ✳ ✳ ✳

# *Voice of the Sarcee*

*I* met Victoria Juliette Whitney through my sister-in-law Kathleen Hyatt who lived at Priddis. "Victoria was a fine woman, she was the first neighbor to call on me when we moved to Priddis. She even took me out and showed me her best berry picking spots!" said Kathleen. This was typical of Victoria who helped not only her Native people but contributed much to the Calgary community. She was a member and president of the Westos Wanderers Group of the Women's Institute of Priddis, the first member of St. Patrick's Church, Midnapore and a member of St. Mary's Church, Calgary.

She was born in a log cabin on the Sarcee Indian Reserve in 1891. Her father George Hodgson, a buffalo hunter, moved north and south with the weather and the herds and became an interpreter and the first farm instructor on the Sarcee Reserve Staff. His wife was Cree, so Victoria was born a Metis. But when she married John One Spot of the Sarcee in 1916 she became one of them, loved and respected by all.

Her father and mother strongly believed in education so Victoria graduated from grade school at Midnapore, from grade 12 at Sacred Heart convent and in 1911 was one of the first Native girls to get a teacher's certificate from the Calgary Normal School. She taught school for a few years and later attended the Calgary Business College. Victoria Whitney was a wonderful storyteller and although she was small of stature she immediately commanded attention, especially when she gave the following address titled

*My People.* She gave this speech when asked at functions and gave me a copy of it when we met.

*Victoria Whitney on the Sarcee reserve*

"The Sarcees are a division of the Beaver tribe of Northern Alberta and originally were a part of the Athabaskan Nation which extends across the whole of Northern Canada. Prior to 1877 no accurate history can be obtained of the Sarcee Indian. However, tribal legend tells us of the crossing of the Athapaskan Nation onto this continent by the Berring Strait. Also legend tells how the Beaver tribe split to give us our present Sarcee Indians.

One day a chief of the Beaver tribe in an idle moment, shot an arrow through a dog belonging to one of his braves. A quarrel ensued and this led to a fight in which the entire tribe participated. After a great many braves were killed a truce was called. However, by this time the situation had become so aggravated that a portion of the tribe decided to break away and find a new home. This they did, drifting south onto the plains of the Saskatachewan River and so became our Sarcees.

No one knows how many hundreds of years ago this happened but the Sarcees became part of the Plains Indians, roaming and hunting the entire length and breadth of the prairies. Before 1700, when horses first reached Central Canada, the plains was a fairly peaceful area because the Indians wandered on foot in small bands and used very primitive weapons. Then, with the introduction of horses and firearms, steel tomahawks and knives, everything was changed. War became a sport. What spurred the Indian on was a thirst for glory, not for blood. It was as honorable to steal an enemy's horse as to take his scalp.

Although the Sarcees were a small tribe in comparison with the Blackfoot and the Crees, they had the name of being a brave and warlike people with whom the neighboring nations were always desirous of being on peaceful terms. In fighting they would often face ten times their own numbers.

As well as being excellent warriors, the Sarcees were excellent beaver and buffalo hunters. Buffalo and antelope were their main sources of food. The buffalo was the staff of life. From its flesh came nearly all their food, from its hide they obtained covers for their tents, shields, saddles, bags to hold their pemmican and clothing; from the bones they fashioned various tools. Pursuit of the buffalo was the principal occupation of every man and youth in the community and a failure in the hunt meant starvation and death. The last buffalo hunt by the Sarcees was held in 1882 just south of the present day agency.

In early years the Sarcees, like other Plains Tribes, were a deeply religious people, placing their hope and trust in an all-powerful deity they called The Maker. They usually thought of him as an old man but believed he might assume any shape he wished. He could appear or disappear in a twinkling of an eye. To their Maker they directed their morning and evening prayers and addressed their oaths. A man would say, "If I lie, may The Maker take my children, but if I tell the truth, may they live long." From some source or another, perhaps from The Maker, the Sarcee believed himself gifted with certain powers – the animals, the rocks and trees being gifted with others. Through contact with these objects in dreams and in visions he believed he could derive great powers or protection from some of the ills of life – power to heal sickness, or immunity from death, or capture in wars.

The Sarcees are a distinct nation and have an entirely different language from any other tribe of the plains – it is very difficult to learn because of the many gutural sounds it contains.

Their Sun Dance was a religious dance put on by a chaste woman who vowed to do so in thanksgiving for having had a request granted. The last Sun Dance held on the Sarcee Reserve was in 1885.

A man was allowed as many wives as he could provide for and they were kind to their old people and generally spoiled their children. When the end of a man's life drew near, close relatives painted the dying man with either red ochre or with marks peculiar to the society of which he was a member, dressed him in his finest clothes and wrapped his other garments in a bundle. Parents and wife put on their oldest clothes, the father unbraided his hair and the mother and wife cut their hair short. The women also gashed their legs with flints or arrow points and frequently cut off a finger at a joint so that if the depth of their sorrow found no outlet in weeping, the pain of the mutilated finger would release their tears. After a short delay to give all the relatives time to join in the funeral train, the relatives placed the dead man, his clothes, weapons and other possessions on a travois, lashed it to one of his horses and dragged it to a tree on a nearby hilltop. There, wrapping the corpse and its clothes in a bundle, they deposited it on high branch, abandoned the weapons and other goods, killed the horse at the foot of the tree and returned to camp. The killing of horses was prohibited after confinement of Indians on reserves but as late as 1919 when they buried an old warrior, Wolf Carrier, the Sarcee secretly killed his favorite horse. I think we all cried more for the horse rather than the dearly departed!

The coming of the white man dealt the Indian two severe blows – disease and gradual loss of his hunting grounds. By the middle of the 19th century the Blackfoot, Bloods, Peigans and Sarcees found themselves backed into Southern Alberta. The Sarcees, always a small band, suffered a great loss in numbers not only from inter-tribal wars, but from epidemics of smallpox and other diseases. Added to that, the starvation that followed the diminishing of the buffalo completely crippled them.

And so it was that in 1877 along with the Blackfoot, Bloods, Peigans, and Blackfoot from Montana, the Sarcee signed Treaty number 7 at Blackfoot Crossing, resigning their hunting ground to the Dominion of Canada on certain conditions, one being that each member of the tribe should receive an annual gratuity of $5. The first annuity was distributed in 1881. The great and glittering gathering of the tribes for the Treaty signing included chiefs, minor chiefs, councillors and medicine men in all their color. Chief Bull Head signed on behalf of the Sarcee Indians and after some shifting around on different sites, decided that the present reservation was the place where his tribe would settle.

The government was not in favor of the site and sent the North West Mounted Police to move the tribe. During the night Chief Bull Head and some of his braves, having heard of the government's plan erected a pole shack. In the morning, when the Police arrived, Chief Bull Head stepped out and announced that this was his home and here he intended to stay. The NWMP backed him up and thus the Sarcee Reserve came into being. It consists of three townships of land adjoining the southwestern boundary of Calgary. It is bounded on the north by the Elbow River and on the south by Fish Creek.

It is interesting to speculate just what was in Chief Bull Head's mind when that tough old warrior settled down on the land for his reserve. It is even more interesting to speculate what he would think if he were alive today and could evaluate in today's terms, the land he chose for his people."

The Sarcee people, now known as the Tsuu T'Ina Nation (whose present chief, Roy Whitney, is Victoria's grandson) have always been active in Calgary life. Old timers will remember them bringing wagon loads of fresh cut Christmas trees from door to door and the women bringing in their delicious fresh Saskatoon berries for sale. During Jack's term as mayor, Dave and Daisy Crowchild were goodwill ambassadors, often included as guests of honor at civic functions. I was at the opening of Crowchild trail on a wintery day when Jack and Chief Crowchild cut the ceremonial ribbon. A fitting tribute to good neighbors.

✳ ✳ ✳ ✳ ✳

*The original version of My People was printed with the kind permission of Victoria Whitney and appeared in Heritage Magazine, Jul/Aug, 1977.*

# The Elbow Valley Playground

*T*he valley was originally the land of the Blackfoot. It was a land of grass that rolled in restless waves to the east and the south as far as the eye could see and stretched to the limits of the imagination. The land was literally black with buffalo when first seen by Father Doucet, who came to establish the first mission to the Indians in 1872. The valley was also heavily timbered along the banks of the Elbow.

Just a year later Sam Livingston came to make his head-quarters nearby. He trapped, hunted buffalo and traded for the next two years. By 1875 he knew this valley was his choice of all the lands he'd seen from Wisconsin to California, along the Mackenzie River and from Edmonton to Winnipeg; so he built a shack for his family and became the first settler in the Elbow Valley. Livingston stood in the valley of the Elbow 5½ kilometres west from where the Elbow River joins the Bow and pulled out his musket. In buckskin breeches, a kerchief knotted at his throat, flaxen hair waving down to his shoulders, Irish eyes full of fun and determination, he fired shots to the north, the south, east and west and claimed. "All that land's mine!"

Sam's granddaughter Nora Sutherland was a friend of mine. "He was determined to farm," she said, "but farming in 1876? It was unheard of here. Old Palliser (Captain John Palliser, the explorer) had sent word back East that nothing would grow on the bleak prairies and cattlemen claimed it was good only for rangeland. It took initiative to promote it as suitable for agriculture but grandfather was just the boy to do it!" His energy and enthusiasm combined with fellow settler John Glenn's knowledge of irrigation, made a winning combination. The practice of irrigating crops was born in Alberta. "By 1879," continued Nora, "he was raising crops of oats yielding 50 bushels per acre and he brought the first mower, rake, binder and threshing machine into this area. In 1883 he built The Big House which was like a side-by-side duplex from the way mother described it, because a school teacher lived in one half. Grandad was very interested in education and insisted that the only way to get 14 children educated was to have a 'live-in' teacher."

A little farther west up the valley were the R. G. Robinsons from San Francisco who bought the Chipman Ranch in 1888. Their address was Elbow Park, NWT, described as "on the Elbow River seven kilometres west of Calgary" ( Fort Calgary). Their ranch buildings were remarkable. One was a three storey barn built into a hillside with the top storey for housing rigs, the second for storing grain and the ground floor of stone used as a dairy. The Robinson's Account Book shows $63.75 worth of potatoes and $7 worth of seed grain bought from Sam Livingston and his nephew, so the Livingston garden was working out to their mutual benefit. The Robinsons had large crews to feed as they had an average of 3 000 horses and cattle on the vast grazing acreage in the Elbow Valley, Bragg Creek, Primez Creek and Fish Creek. Specializing in horses, the ranch imported stallions from England and catered to big ranchers like Pat Burns, who paid $250 for a pair of grey geldings in 1891. They were also farriers and suppliers to the Calgary detachment of the North West Mounted Police.

About the time the Elbow Park Ranch was waxing prosperous, a Calgary liveryman and stable keeper, William Ford, purchased 26.6 acres of the river front from the CPR close to the growing town of Calgary. In the great boom of 1912 this became the Rockcliffe Subdivision containing over 100 homesites. At this time James Stanilon Stocks from Leeds, England came to the valley. He had the same kind of visions for development as John Hextall had for Bowness in the Bow Valley. Stocks built a large English manor house on the banks of the Elbow river. It was complete with butler's pantry, maid's bedroom, billiard room, large family dining, spacious reception hall and seven open fireplaces. There was a large barn and carriage house and sweeping lawns for tennis courts. The house was hardly finished however, when the first World War started and Stocks packed up his family and took the first boat home to fight for Mother England. The home fell to vandals, weather and Ike Ruttle's goats. Ike was a Calgary liveryman and had no idea the goats did anything more than graze on the thick grass outside the house.

It was 1922 when Jack Leslie's father heard the house was for sale. There were remnants of grain stored in the kitchen and all the light fixtures had been ripped from their sockets; the battleship linoleum had been pulled from the kitchen and bathroom floors; the hot water heating system had frozen leaving a welter of broken pipes and a ruined wall. But they bought it because the price was a mere $2 500 with no down payment. Because it was just outside the City Limits taxes were just $6 a year which looked good compared to $300 for a home in the city. "It was something like living in a barn," reminisced Jack, "I remember handing Dad wrenches and hammers as he lay on his back in the small space under the boiler in the basement as he worked to get the heating system working again."

After many years and much hard work the house was back in shape and it too became a home of hospitality, its door always open to scores of members of the Commonwealth Air Training program at nearby Currie Barracks during World War II. Jack remembers coming home unexpectedly on leave to find not one empty bed in the house!

Agnes Leslie's Sunday dinners would have rivaled any of those of the early ranch wives. Her specialty was roast beef with Yorkshire pudding. Not the high, puffy kind, full of air, but a solid sconelike pudding that she cooked around the roast to absorb all the rich flavors of the meat and gravy. This she served with delicious home made mustard pickles. Every other Sunday it was a chicken almost as large as a turkey – one of the Jersey Black Giants that she raised herself. When served with vegetables fresh or home canned from their own prolific garden, and Saskatoon pie for dessert, it was no wonder that the boys of the Air Force never forgot her. The house is still there on the banks of the Elbow just below the 15th hole of the Calgary Golf and Country Club. There as a youth Jack fished errant golf balls out of river holes and sold them back to club members. Next door to the Leslie home Stanilon Stocks had built another fine old English home. In the 1920s Lorenzo L. Smith, a pioneer in the oil industry lived there with his wife and family. In 1936 they sold to William J. Steel, a well known Calgary florist.

* * *

From earliest times the Elbow and its valley had provided a playground for Calgarians – the first hockey or 'shinnie' game recorded in the city was played on the river's ice New Year's day 1888; the first fall race meet was held there in 1890. Cappy Smart (Calgary's famous fireman) and other sportsmen, noting that the Sarcees entertained themselves there every spring and summer with bucking horse contests and races, held an official rodeo in what was known as Moccasin Flats, or the Mission area in 1896.

Although city growth by the 1920s had eaten away most of Elbow Park and Mission, leaving only a small area between the river and the base of Brittania hill for the annual Riverdale Stampede, the long stretch of valley from Sandy Beach up past the Leslies and as far as the old Robinson Ranch remained a well-used and loved playground for the children of Calgary. The fields and hills were green with grasses and tall evergreens and brilliant colors in early summer with dozens of varieties of wild flowers. Family berry picking expeditions were treasured days of hard work providing an excuse for lavish picnics and the reward of pails full of choke-cherries and saskatoons for winter jams, jellies and pies.

Teachers took their classes up the valley for picnics in summer and for skating parties far up the river in winter. Many families had an old horse or two and the Leslie, Campbell, Quint, Howard, Gregg and Humphrey children ranged up as far as Twin bridges in a game they called "Chase," like "Red Light, Green Light" but on horseback.

The spring of 1929 brought a series of events that were to spell disaster to the valley playground. The City Reservoir over on the Bow became so low that some districts were without water. In June both the Bow and the Elbow rampaged in the worst flood since 1902 which was soon followed by a scorching summer that brought on water rationing.

Panic struck in October when four cases of typhoid were traced to some springs on the Walker Estate in East Calgary and worried citizens lined up for water from the spring above Riley Park. City council, after listening to dozens of plans to alleviate their water problems chose the one that was most economical and most quickly constructed – Glenmore Dam. All who loved the valley read with unbelieving eyes and sinking hearts the engineer's report which said Calgary should draw its water supply in the future entirely from the Elbow River, a reservoir covering 900 acres of land, held behind a dam 60 feet high (18 metres), 80 feet long (24 m) at its crest and 40 feet long (12 m) at the river levels. The report continued, "That land is, in our opinion, of little value for any other purpose than that proposed." *That land* of Sam Livingston's prolific gardens, the old Robinson Ranch, *that land* for riding, berrypicking and hiking. The dam itself would be less than a kilometre above the homes of J. C. Leslie and Lorenzo Smith. Mr. Hornibrook, a candidate for alderman in the fall election, voiced public concern that building the dam just 5 ½ kilometres from city hall could constitute a risk to the residents of Elbow Park and the southern section of the city. But he was defeated and the water by-law passed with a handsome majority.

Only after Mayor Andy Davison turned the sod to commence construction in July 1930 and the bulldozers scarred the countryside and the cement spillways grew ominously higher did many Elbow Park residents become alarmed. When the cost of land acquisition rose from the estimated $150 000 to $350 000 there was a judicial inquiry conducted by Judge Ewing. "We were all on the carpet, every one of us," said Pansy Pue, alderman at the time, "but the judge subpoenaed 'rumormongers' and brought in a report exonerating the mayor, council and all involved in land transactions." Meanwhile, during construction on the dam, one worker, Hans Jenson, unused to working over water, fell in when he was assigned a job over the pounding spume and drowned in the flotsam and jetsam swirling around at the bottom.

The Leslie boys and their friends soon turned the construction work into adventure. Tow heads glistened in the summer sun as they laboriously carted home the used cribbing from the cement work to build a tree house, and when the steep cement spillways were poured the children slid down them on pieces of cardboard!

As stately spruce fell to bucksaws and whipsaws the waters rose to reach Sam Livingston's Big House. One part of the home was moved to the City's nursery on 14th street and the other part was bought and taken by Milton Williams to his farm at the top of the hill. The waters continued to rise until by the end of 1932 the entire 900 acres of the valley were flooded.

For a long time it looked as though the easily accessible Elbow Valley playground was gone forever but in 1962 a new concept was born when an anonymous donor gave the city $150 000. This sparked a *City of Calgary - Glenbow Foundation* project resulting in what we now know as Heritage Park. The idea of Calgarians picnicing and playing in 60 acres of land surrounding Glenmore Reservoir (the city water supply) did not appeal to all members of council,

*Glenmore dam under construction, 1931*

some of whom, like alderman Ernie Starr, objected to "people washing their feet in my drinking water." But there were also on council those who understood that swimming would not be allowed and a filtering plant stood right on the banks of the reservoir to purify our water. Jack and aldermen Grant MacEwan, Bill Dickie and Roy Deyell were able to swing a majority vote to develop the area into an historic pioneer village and allow a base for Calgary sailors.

Today thousands of Calgarians and their visitors enjoy picnicing and playing among reminders of our past in the Valley of the Elbow.

\* \* \* \* \*

# Christmas Spirit

*T*he Venerable Archdeacon Swanson had seen Christmases in the Yukon, Victoria, Vancouver, Lethbridge and Toronto and he had many stories to tell about his days in each but as we talked he believed his most poignant Christmas story happened here in Calgary.

It was a cold Christmas Eve about 1935 when Harry and his friend Pete were finishing their Club Christmas Hamper calls on the edge of the city. As they came to the last house on their list they noticed they would end up with one extra hamper.

"What'll we do, take it back?" asked Pete.

"I suppose so," said Harry. But as they were leaving the grateful household they asked, "Any other family nearby who can use a hamper?"

Their mother answered, "Well, there are new people just over that way. I don't know them but they have three or four children". Off went Pete and Harry. They knocked on the door of the little cottage, introduced themselves and offered the hamper.

"Oh thank you sirs, thank you!" said the mother, "our children will have a real Christmas now."

"How many are there?" the boys asked.

"Four altogether," the mother replied.

Harry looked around and saw the husband and three open-mouthed kiddies. "Where's the other?" he asked.

"Oh, he's in the shed."

"In the shed?" exclaimed Harry, "Where?"

"I'll show you," said the father and led Harry out to a little lean-to nailed on the house. In it was a bed and in the bed, white and wan, lay a little boy. Harry was an ex TB patient and knew the problem as soon as he sniffed the air. He greeted the little chap and turned to the father and said, "I'll be back on Wednesday morning."

When that morning came he was back with a carpenter. In two days a new lean-to had been built, a new bed provided with new, warm blankets and a big glass window installed. A doctor came and checked the boy's lungs and domestic arrangements.

Harry never told a soul and cautioned Pete not to talk about it either. But Pete confided in Archdeacon Swanson. Before that Christmas hamper call was over Harry had given no less than $1 800 to help the small boy with TB.

Said Archdeacon Swanson, "That is Christmas. Not just one day, but a philosophy of service."

✳ ✳ ✳ ✳ ✳

# "Get 'em while they're hot!"

Roy Beavers had quite a sales pitch at the 1908 Calgary Industrial Exhibition (forerunner to the present day Calgary Exhibition and Stampede).

"Come one, come all! See the greatest snake show on earth!"

As the crowd edged nervously forward to see a huge boa constrictor slithering down and around the head and shoulders of his partner Recker, Roy would sell food.

"Here pardner, have a hot dog while you watch that wonderman Recker and his trained live snakes!" Enveloped in the pungent smoke of frying onions, hot dogs and potatoes on a huge griddle, Roy shovelled the sizzling food into buns for hungry fairgoers, "Here y'are pardner, all brown and piping hot!"

Roy Beavers was having the time of his young life but he was a long way from home. He had graduated from High School at Whitehall, Illinois in 1904 and was working for ten cents an hour putting handles on churns and jugs at the Whitehall Sewerpipe and Stoneware Factory, when Recker approached him, "Hi Roy, why don't you come in with me on this hot dog stand of mine? I'm goin' to the Louisiana Purchase Centennial Exposition in St. Louis and you'd make a heck of a lot more money there than you'll ever make here, besides think of the fun we'd have!" So Roy was lured into the world of hustling, sawdust and fairground food.

He and Recker spent the next four years on the fair circuit, which started in Florida, swung up through Western Canada for the summer, then over to Vancouver and back down to Florida for the winter.

*Roy Beavers' snake show, 1908*

The only drawback to this kind of life was that it took Roy away from the girl he had been courting – Evelyn (nicknamed Lina), the daughter of Whitehall's town doctor. As she was becoming more and more impatient, the only solution to Roy was to marry the girl and take her along as cashier.

The circuit took them through Calgary two or three times. The free-wheeling town of those days appealed to both Lina and Roy, so when the show hit Calgary again in 1911 they decided to stay. Soon the name Beavers became synonymous with food both at the Fair Grounds and in downtown Calgary. So it remained for over 50 years.

\* \* \*

Roy Beavers was of medium build, athletic and interested in sports and always serious about business. He had prematurely white hair and hazel eyes that twinkled with fun, especially when he was spinning a tall yarn – like this one he inevitably told on pheasant hunting expeditions, "I had a pooch who could drive pheasants into a hole in the ground. Then he would put a large paw over the cavity and wait for me. When I came up he would release the birds one by one simply by lifting one paw!" He told the tale so often he thought nothing of spinning it off to a young man near Brooks one day and to his horror it appeared as news in the district pages of *The Herald*!

He was also a superstitious man. Not only was Friday, especially Friday the 13th, an unlucky day, Roy knew his lucky days and his lucky number – 11. He married Lina at 11AM on the 11th month of 1909. He opened his first restaurant, the Club Café in Calgary at 11 AM on the 11th day of the 11th month in 1911 at 111 - 8th Avenue East. When he moved the Club Café west, his new address was 111 - 8th Avenue West. It, too, opened its doors for business on all the "elevens."

Lina, Roy's partner in life and business, was not a dot over 4 feet, 11 inches but had energy and generosity enough for two her size right up to the day she died in 1973.

She was expecting a baby that first year in Calgary and she and Roy lived in one room where she rented a sewing machine and made all her baby clothes and Christmas presents. They moved into a house just before the baby came. There, Lina took in boarders and nursed not only her own baby, but the one next door. She even found time to make hand-dipped chocolates as well as prepare three meals a day for Roy and his partners as they worked to get their new restaurant, the Club Café ready to open.

The Club Café was just a lurch and a holler from the "longest bar in the world" at the Alberta Hotel and figured largely in Calgary's early days. The Club Café was the favorite eating place for many well-known figures including abstemious lawyer R. B. Bennett, witty Irish lawyer Paddy Nolan, grocer John Irwin and, in later years, Bert Baker, who became a president of the Calgary Stampede. Baker remembers, "Roy really loved to talk to all his customers."

*Counter Club Café, Roy Beavers in right foreground*

Bob Edwards, Calgary's noted (or notorious) newspaper man was also a frequent and welcome customer. He was remembered by Lina Beavers as "a sober and pleasant gentleman." Well, not always. On those rather frequent occasions when "John Barleycorn" got the better of him,

Edwards would razz Roy about his "old grub Café" and had to be hustled out.

Hi-jinks were popular at Fair times and during the 1923 Stampede a cowboy actually rode into the Club Café on his horse going all the way around the counter, while one of Roy's helpers, an effeminate little man with ruffles on his sleeve, scuttled along behind with a broom and dustpan.

Roy aided the community in many ventures. In 1927 when the Boy Scouts collected a record number of toys at their annual Christmas Toy Shop Movies. They had to work right through the afternoon sorting the donated toys, so Roy invited the whole gang into his Café. "Give them anything they want from turkey down, and lots of it," he instructed the chef. That was typical of Roy's generosity and his awareness of community needs. Small wonder he was known to thousands of Calgarians as "Pappy Beavers."

The Beavers sold the Club Café in 1944 and bought the White Lunch Cafe at 225 - 8th Avenue West and then McCrohan's located opposite to the Palliser Hotel. It was 1948 before Roy succumbed yet again to the catering call of the midway. This time he took on all of the catering for the Calgary Exhibition & Stampede Board which included serving in Fort Calgary House, the old Victoria Arena and at all the Prize Fights Events with a wagon-portable stand.

Serving everyone from Queen Elizabeth to the performers in the side-shows, to a "Feed for the Big Boss and his Missus" (the Governor General Viscount and Lady Alexander), Roy and his staff catered to the hearty appetites at the Stampede Grounds continuously for twenty years until 1968, when the Stampede Board bought out his business and equipment when he retired.

Roy and Lina Beavers were fun-loving, gregarious and generous. Their home became the hub of a growing community, some of it their own (by 1920 they had three sons). Halloween meant giving out the biggest balls of popcorn any of the kids had ever seen and Christmas meant "open house" to hundreds of friends.

The Beavers were among the first of the thousands of Americans who poured into Calgary. As Lina herself said, "We had a lot of hard times and it was hard work, but the work always seemed like fun. We thought we'd make a little money and go back to the States. But we never went back, and we never wanted to."

*****

# *Grub Pile*

**Green Grass Salad** . . . . . . . . . . . . . . . . . . . . . . . . salad

**Berries** . . . . . . . . . . . . . . . . . . . . . . . . . boiled beans

**Sow Belly** . . . . . . . . . . . . . . . . . . . . boiled side pork

**Barbecued Buffalo** . . . . . . . . . . . our neighbor's beef

**Punk and Axle Grease** . . . . . . . . . . rolls and butter

**Spuds** . . . . . . . . . . . . . . . . . . . . . . . . . . . . . . potatoes

**Plenty of Red Paint** . . . . . . . . . . . . . . . . . . ketchup

**C.P.R.Strawberries** . . . . . . . . . . . . . . . . . . . . prunes

**Sinkers** . . . . . . . . . . . . . . . . . . . . . . . . . . . . donuts

**Pie** . . . . . . . . . . . . . . . any kind as long as it's apple

**Java, black or**
**with sand and cow** . . . . coffee with milk and sugar

✳ ✳ ✳ ✳ ✳

*Translated Beavers' menu for Viscount and Lady Alexander,*
*who appreciated Roy's humor.*

# S.S. *Calgaric*

$A$s school children from a low income family in the 'dirty thirties,' my brothers, sisters and I went to the free school dentist at City Hall. There, we were entranced by the wide winding staircases and the open balcony gallery on the third and fourth floors where we could stand and look down on the people on the main floor. It was like looking through a telescope backwards. Everything looked rounder and smaller. Some of the boys did more than look – they spat!

Near the Mayor's office was the model of *S. S. Calgaric*, proud ship of the White Star Canadian service. We pressed our noses hard upon the glass case for we had never seen, nor did we ever expect to see, a real-life ocean liner. She looked long and sleek and luxurious when she became the latest in the White Star fleet in 1927 and was christened "Calgaric" in honor of this booming western city.

Landlocked Calgarians were excited by the honor and decided to make a presentation to the *S. S. Calgaric's* master and her crew when she docked at Montreal. Consequently, Mayor Fred Osborne and C.O. Smith, president of the Calgary Board of Trade and former *Herald* editor, were there on May 17, 1927 to watch the *S. S. Calgaric* sail up the St. Lawrence and into port. The same evening a huge dinner crowd was welcomed aboard the 16 000 ton vessel by P. A. Curry, general manager of the shipping company. Following a sumptuous meal, Mayor Osborne presented on behalf of the citizens of Calgary, a buffalo head emblazoned with a silver plaque. Banqueting guests aboard that luxury liner would have been astounded to learn that spit, polish and paint had successfully hidden the fact that the S. S. *Calgaric* had started life as the S. S. *Orca*, launched in 1919 as one of the largest cargo carrying ships to sail out of Liverpool. She was also one of the ugliest.

Originally designed as a passenger-cargo vessel, she was placed into service without passenger decks, with a cruiser stern, a single funnel, two very tall masts and an enormous cargo capacity. No one would have guessed that her maiden voyage as the *S.S.Orca* was fraught with all the drama and violence of *Mutiny on the Bounty*.

Wallace G. Carter settled in Calgary in 1948. Originally from Australia he boarded the *S.S. Orca* in 1922 as assistant purser. From his partially completed manuscript that he gave me, early voyages of the ship are revealed. On its first voyage, commanded by Captain Kite, the *S.S. Orca* disembarked from Cardiff with "255 colored civilians who had been removed from gaols in England." Then to make matters worse, at Havre 80 French prisoners were put aboard with an escort of 16 inexperienced young men. At the Captain's insistence, "the guard" (guards on duty) was placed in the ship's care. However it was not long before several of the prisoners incited mutiny. Wrote Carter, "They were placed in cells but the remainder of the men openly defied the Captain. Finally, when the guard attacked, they opened fire killing one man and wounding another. Extra armed guards, with the assistance of the ship's officers, watched over the prisoners continuously. Later the Captain mixed with the men, unarmed himself, and endeavored to reason with them to restore law and order before more of their number were killed. He was indeed a brave man."

The second voyage had problems too. Carter wrote: "Commanded by Captain Beale we left Liverpool, our end destination Valparaiso, Chile. Arriving at New York we tied up at Pier 43 where it was so bitterly cold that blocks of ice floated around the ship. We loaded coal from lighters and freight from the pier warehouses and some extremely valuable Holstein cattle including one bull, "Old Bill," worth more than $6 000. My first impression of New York was decidedly unpleasant and quite frankly I was glad when we were due to pull out for Baltimore. However, about an hour before we cast off I saw several of the firemen and greasers leaving the ship, dressed in their shore clothes and carrying their bags. Within 15 minutes the entire engine room crew, except for the two senior men, about 65 in all, were sitting in a line on the dock determined not to continue the voyage unless their demands were met by the captain. The company's agents on shore managed to round up a motley bunch of 30 men, termed 'runners' to help get the ship to Baltimore. At Baltilmore, where we went alongside at Locust Point, we sank some 18 inches or so into the mud but thankfully suffered no damage. Here we were received by port authorities and city officials in grand style as the *Orca* was, at that time, the longest vessel to have entered the port. We took on board about 50 men to replace the deserters. They were the 'sweepings of the dockside' and from the time they came on board until our arrival at Callao life on the ship – day and night – was hellish. The officers all carried revolvers and threatened to use them any time a man approached the bridge or commenced to make trouble anywhere. The ship's doctor was the only officer the men would allow amongst them and that was only to tend those badly in need of medical attention. But he never carried a gun when tending them. Once at port the ringleaders were taken ashore and placed in gaol to cool down."

The *S. S. Orca* served the Pacific Steam Navigation Company as a freighter from 1920 to 1922. That year she returned to the builders to be transformed into a modern passenger liner and was rechristened the *S. S. Calgaric*. The model of the *S. S. Calgaric* still stands on display at City Hall.

✳ ✳ ✳ ✳ ✳

# House of Two Dreams

$T$he house began as the epitome of the dream of John Hextall, a gentleman who came to Calgary from England in 1908. While staying at the Palliser Hotel he explored the countryside looking for suitable ranch property. He immediately became enthusiastic over the natural beauties of the valley of the Bow about six miles above the junction of the Elbow and the Bow Rivers. He saw more than broad plains, stands of spruce and willow, hills and the river – he saw a vision of stately homes graciously fronting on the Bow and folded into the hills. He saw a whole community with its own power, water and all the amenities of life as well as its pleasures, including a golf and country club. He returned to England and formed the Bowness Land Development Company selling lots to enthralled Englishmen for as high as $10 000, sight unseen!

He built five large English style homes in the valley. His own Tudor mansion was the most palatial. When I first saw the house I could imagine how guests swept up a long, curved driveway to the front door and entered a large reception hall where a fire burned in a brick fireplace to the left. Visitors' eyes would be caught by a long staircase of gleaming oak with three wide landings, carved banisters and matching wrought iron lamps hanging from oak-beamed ceilings. Off the reception hall was a handsome oak-lined library. Downstairs was another fireplace in the grand ballroom where an orchestra played on a raised platform at one end of the room. Plush chairs stood against the walls and the blazing chandelier cast the shadows of the elegantly dressed dancers on the paneled oak walls. The house became famous for its parties. Rather than attempting the two hour buggy trip back to the city in the dark, guests often stayed overnight in the two great bedroom wings, one for ladies and another for gentlemen. Imagine the quilts on the Hextall beds! Land sales were booming until late 1913 when war clouds gathering in Europe prompted the British backers of the development company to withdraw their support and John Hextall, the man who dreamed of Calgary's first perfect suburb, faced bankruptcy and left to enlist with the British armed forces.

*Hextall's home, interior view of hall, 1928*

After standing for some time in isolated splendor, Hextall's mansion was bought by the Seventh Day Adventist Church for a sanitarium. It wasn't until 1926 that the deserted house was discovered by Reverend George Wood a man with a different dream.

Reverend George Wood also had come from Britain in 1908. He was born in Greenock, Scotland where little is known of his early life except that he spent a number of years on the staff of the Quarrier Orphan Homes at Bridge of Weir. He settled with his wife and baby in Melfort, Saskatchewan.

In 1910 the lovely young wife of Reverend Wood was lighting the lamps in their tiny manse house. One lamp glowed softly and she moved to light the other. But a careless grocer had sold her gasoline instead of kerosene and the lamp exploded, killing her. Because of this tragedy Reverend Wood appealed to the church authorities for a move to Alberta for a fresh start with his three year old daughter Ann. A cheery man, mustached, curly-haired, with a broad Scottish accent and always seeming to be smiling, Wood was a popular minister in his new church at Innisfail, Alberta.

In 1914 the effects of World War I hit the community. The wife of one of the town's men suddenly died when he was waiting to go overseas to the ward. Her death meant that their three children would be parentless. Compassionate leave was unknown at the time so the soldier begged George Wood to look after his young orphans. George agreed. Less than a month later, other orphaned children were brought for him to look after. Within six months he was caring for 30 orphans with the help of his widowed mother, then in her seventies. After searching desperately for room to house his expanding family, George rented the abandoned Innisfail Hospital. Children kept arriving until he had 100 orphans in what he called Wood's Christian Home. Forced to give up the ministry to look after his "family," financial support became a pressing problem. Relatives across the country and particularly a sister and brother-in-law in Calgary helped enormously but he constantly had to appeal to the community for funds.

His life brightened considerably when a childhood sweetheart, Annie Jarvie, visited her Calgary relatives. George Wood was obviously smitten anew but could not find his tongue to say so before escorting Annie to the train for home. He moped around his sister's home for three days, preaching at Calgary churches in the evening to raise funds, then pacing the floor during the daytime until his sister finally said, "Why don't you send a telegram?" Annie received the telegram just as she was walking up the gangplank of a ship in Montreal. She got off and returned to be the "mother" of the "family."

In 1926, on one of his money-raising forays into Calgary, George Wood discovered Hextall's old home. After pleading with the Adventist Church to let him use the mansion for his family they finally agreed to sell the home and its surrounding acreage of beautiful grass and trees for $18 000 without interest. That was a fraction of its 1912 cost of $65 000 but George managed to close the negotiations by putting up his life insurance policy for the debt.

*Hextall's house, later known as Wood's Christian Home*

As soon as Calgarians became aware of the project they began to help. George, of course, had no car and as the Home was at Bowness, some ten miles out on the outskirts of the city, he would cleverly ask other ministers or influential Calgarians to drive him out. Once they saw the hundred happy children, they would offer help. Dr. J. V. Follett took care of hundreds of Wood's children through the years, free of charge. Local dentists did likewise. Support came from churches of all faiths, lodges and service clubs. About November 1927 an organization heard of the needs of the home and within a short time had $2 000 to hand over. That marked the turning point in the history of the home and the beginning of a period of interest from the community that finally cleared off all indebtedness, put the property in first class shape and allowed the construction of a boy's dormitory by 1930.

Thanks to writers like Kipling and Dickens the word 'orphanage' conjured up for most people pictures of dreary institutions full of ogres and unhappiness so George Wood never used the words *orphan* or *orphanage*. He had a unique way of handling youngsters – he persuaded boys to hoe potatoes by suggesting they "tickle the toes o' the taties" and girls to wash dishes by saying, "I just wanted tae tell you there's a sinkful o' durrrty dishes wanting tae meet up wi' some bonnie lassies like you!"

George Wood invited a few Calgary citizens to act on a Board of Trustees who in October 1928 raised over $12 000. Just when it seemed the difficult days of finance were over, George Wood died after a short illness on November 27, 1928. Years of unceasing strain and anxiety had taken their toll. With tremendous support from the Calgary community this gentle man's concept of a home for parentless youngsters continued even after his death and that of Mrs. Wood. It was estimated that some 5 000 children passed through the loving hands of the Woods.

Over the years, from 1935, the average number of children in the home had been around 90 to 100, but by 1965 was reduced to about 60. This was followed by a change to caring for disturbed children as other agencies took over the work of abandoned youths. In the early 1970s the house, with the addition of several cottages, was being used for these disturbed children. About 1973 I was asked to replace Wilma Hansen, long time worker for children, on the Board of Wood's Christian Homes. After innumerable evaluations and studies the Homes were soon operating under the Provincial Department of Health. Meetings were held at the lovely home.

When I returned from a short trip out of the country in the spring of 1975, I found that the old Hextall Home had been bulldozed down. Outraged, I resigned. Evidently there had been a minor fire in the building which led to the discovery that the foundation of the building was in poor condition. The organization of Wood's Christian Homes would continue to assist needy and disturbed adolescents.

I felt then, and still do, that if Calgarians had been appealed to, just as they were in George Wood's day, they would have responded with funds for restoration. I cannot think of another house in our city that had the historical and emotional background of this one. A long planned Reunion Picnic went ahead at the site shortly after demolition and my feelings of shock and sadness were reflected in the faces of all. They came from as far away as Saskatoon, Priddis and Canmore to meet with those living in the Calgary area. Memories spanned from 1926 to 1969 and included happy stories about being married there, the dreaded visit of the dentist who had a chair set up, visits by Calgary barbers and of fantastic Christmas parties and concerts sponsored by Calgary service clubs. A particularly poignant story came from one man who remembered walking across the ice of the frozen Bow River to visit his mother in the TB Sanatorium on the other side. As he gazed down into the rubble another man murmured, "I can't believe it's gone. I remember the first time I saw our Woods Home ... I jumped out of the car and yelled, 'We've come to the king's palace!'"

*****

# *"Ride 'em Cowboy!"*

I must confess that when I went to interview Herman
Linder some 20 years ago I thought of cowboys as rather
unkempt, traveling from town to town, sleeping with their
horses and some of the girls that I saw admiring them
down at the Stampede barns. But Herman was, and looked
like, a gentleman. In fact he was so slight and soft voiced
when he began "rodeoing," seasoned cowboys didn't
think he'd have a chance. He proved them wrong – he was
balance and grace personified in the saddle.

*Herman Linder bull riding at Calgary stampede*

From 1929 to 1939 he won no less than 22 titles at the Calgary Stampede breaking all definitions of an "all-round hand". He won championships for Canadian bucking horse riding, bareback bucking horse riding, the Canadian and North American all-round cowboy, steer riding and the Canadian bronc riding with-saddle. Small wonder that he became the "Wayne Gretsky" to the young boys of the 1930s, including Jack. They were thrilled by his feats on the saddle. But in 1939, at the height of his fame, Herman Linder quit rodeo. Throughout the 1940s and '50s Herman found he couldn't get rodeo out of his system and stayed close to the game, buying strings of horses for large rodeo outfits and subsequently helping to stage small rodeos at Cardston, Macleod and Lethbridge. He then moved up to the larger shows in Vancouver, Edmonton and Winnipeg.

Jack, as chairman of Calgary's Canada Centennial Committee had been successful in promoting a miniature rodeo from Calgary to be a show at Montreal's Expo '67. He was delighted when the search for a producer turned up Herman Linder. Linder's flair for the theatric (like Guy Weadick, cowboy-turned-promoter) and experience with rodeos made him the ideal choice.

Picture the scene at Expo's Stadium – a whole herd of Texas long-horns storm into the centre of the arena where they surge about; veteran chuck-wagon racer Tom Dorchester dashes in with a chuckwagon, complete with tent and stove; real Alberta cowboys on their graceful cutting horses round the cattle up and lead them into a holding circle, then drift toward a campfire where Wilf Carter is strumming on his guitar. It's a perfect cameo of the Old West in the heart of Montreal. Said Linder, "Then we burst loose with a rootin'-tootin' rodeo – bareback riding, bronc riding, roping and steer decorating. It was so cold you couldn't have paid me to sit in those stands! But I watched and those Quebecers never left till the last calf was tied."

✳ ✳ ✳ ✳ ✳

# Southern Alberta's "Bob Hope"

*J*ack and I were persuaded by friends to join in square dancing when the craze hit Calgary about 1950. As we diffidently took our four left feet into the auditorium of Elbow Park School, we peeked in the door to see a slender, grey-haired woman (not really handsome – rugged would perhaps describe her better) sitting before an upright piano waiting for her cue from caller Collier Maberley.

"Take your partners!" sang out Collier and suddenly such a toe-tapping, hand-clapping beat thumped out of that old piano that before we knew it, we were dancing. The pianist was Ma Trainor, who for over thirty-five years, played for southern Alberta dancers.

We later were amazed to learn that "Ma," properly named Josephine, began as a serious pianist after graduating from Notre Dame Academy, taught at St. Dunstan's University and was pianist for several Lieutenant-Governors at Government House in Charlottetown, Prince Edward Island. She was born in that city in 1875 and was a musical prodigy by age five. Music was the great influence in her life until romance came in the guise of John Trainor, a contractor whom she married in 1904.

Talking with the Trainor's daughter Gertrude McIlhargey, I got the feeling that her mother intended to settle down and become a typical (for those days) housewife, but she simply had too much energy and initiative. So the very first summer Josephine landed a job "demonstrating" for a flour mill in a stall at Calgary's first Stampede.

"Demonstrating really meant handing out pamphlets", Gertrude laughingly recalled. But undaunted, Josephine carried on with cheerful talk in free moments with the man in the stall across the way who happened to run a music store. When the man received a request for a dance pianist from Senator James Lougheed he referred Mrs. Trainor, who agreed to play on the basis of "no fee unless satisfactory."

"A cheer went up after the first waltz and next thing I knew the Lougheed boys had talked their mother into hiring me for their next *dansant!*" She played frequently at the Lougheed mansion with her newly formed band. One evening at their home Edward, Price of Wales danced into the wee hours of the morning with Lougheed's daughter Dorothy, who was an excellent dancer.

Before long when a town had a celebration of any kind they wanted Ma Trainor and her band to play. The name of her band changed frequently from the sedate *Mrs. Trainor's Orchestra* to *Ma Trainor's Old Time Hillbillies* to *Ma Trainor's Hell Bellies Orchestra*. So she and her group trouped all over Alberta, from Reid Hill to Lincoln to Carstairs, Mossleigh, Duchess, Patricia, Cayley, Carbon and Gleichen.

Despite the fact that she started with the "cream" of Calgary society and hers was the official dance band at the Palliser Hotel for 15 years, Mrs. Trainor and her orchestras played for every level of society – The Tipperary Club, The Brotherhood of Trainmen, the Daughters and Maids of England, and every Monday night for 12 years for the Yorkshire Society of Calgary.

But Ma's self-professed "greatest pleasure" came when playing for the service men and women of both Great Wars who dubbed her "Ma." From 1914 to 1918 the entire proceeds from her benefit concerts went to *The Calgary Herald's Tobacco Fund* for soldiers' comforts. They loved her at dances held by the Women's Patriotic Society and the Red Cross. She gave generously of her time, talent and money to the Sunshine Santa Claus Fund during the 1930s.

She was a veteran ballot counter at election times and when hostilities broke out in 1939 she lost no time in organizing weekly dances for service personnel at the Knights of Columbus Hall. There, Ma played for those young men and women every single Sunday night for the next six years. Small wonder she received more than 500 cards and letters from all over the world on her 75th birthday.

*Ma Trainor and servicemen and women, c. 1941*

Victor Ager recalled playing with Ma's band. He played sax and drums with Ma and other band members through the years – Harry Hodgson, Billy Wells, Fred Longacre, Joe Bosch, George Evans, Johnny Petro, Jack Kellaway, George Grefe, Clarence Foss, Billy Guerard and Joe Ferguson. Ferguson "played first violin and chewed 'snoose' (tobacco) for which Ma would have to put down a piece of paper near the piano at each concert or dance so that each time Joe spat he never missed a tissue or a beat."

At one time she had an all-woman orchestra and always encouraged women to join her. But it wasn't easy to keep up with Josephine Trainor. Mrs. Josh Henthorn (on drums and saxophone) recalled, "One time we were playing at Beiseker when the wind caught my drum and sent it rolling across the prairie!"

Another time, CJCJ's Scoop Turner remembered a night that "It was so foggy, Neville York, one of the band members, was lying out on a fender of the car directing the driver! We pushed and pulled and dug ourselves out of mud and snowdrifts to get to a gig and did the same to get back home after the farmers had danced till dawn and finally went home to milk the cows."

I suppose it was her Tuesday night stints of "old time" music on radio station CJCJ that made Ma Trainor so well known throughout the southern part of the province. In the bleak days of the '30s when there was no money, any free entertainment was welcome. Country people danced in their homes to her music or, on those rare occasions when they came to the city, they crowded into CJCJ's small studio in the basement of the Renfrew Building to watch their star perform in person. Their enthusiastic applause and toe tapping added excitement to the programs.

I think Ma Trainor's daughter Gertrude summed up her mother most accurately, "She had a marvellous sense of humor and a real dedication to the servicemen for whom she played for so many years. I think mother was southern Alberta's Bob Hope!"

✳ ✳ ✳ ✳ ✳

# On the Banks of the Bow

*I*n the development from fort to town to city, the Bow has been the backbone of Calgary's commerce.

As early as 1886, the Eau Claire sawmill was built on its banks near what is now Centre Street. In its heyday, the mill turned out three carloads of lumber daily and processed from three to five million feet of spruce, jackpine and fir which floated down the Bow. Log drives were conducted every spring until 1944. In the beginning the fast-flowing Bow caused problems for the lumber company. I read recently in *Glenbow* magazine that Peter A. Prince (manager of the sawmills), in an effort to regulate the water needed for the running of the mills, blasted out the peninsula that stuck out into the Bow. The water stream could now be controlled; the result was Prince's Island.

Now, 100 years later Eau Claire market stands on the site of this saw mill. But when it was still a mill, from this successful enterprise I. K. Kerr (president of the Eau Claire & Bow River Lumber Company) and manager Peter Prince organized the Calgary Iron Works and, most important to women turning their washing machines by hand, the two men provided the first source of electrical power to Calgary.

Using a primitive water wheel on the unpredictable Bow River, the team managed to provide lights during high water flow periods in the summer. The lights dimmed when the river was low and homes fell into pitch blackness when there was heavy ice or an ice jam.

*Eau Claire saw mills, 1890s*

In 1906, the City started a competing distribution system and in 1938, took over the original distribution system which it operates to this day, with much of its power supplied by Calgary Power from Bearspaw, Kananaskis, Spray and Seebe dams, all on the Bow and its tributaries.

The Bow River figured in the first grand civic centre proposed for Calgary. In the real estate boom of 1912-13, City Council decided that if Calgary was to live up to its predicted potential it must have its face lifted.

From Thomas Mawson & Sons (recognized as one of the leading engineering firms in Britain) came Thomas Mawson himself to present a town plan that would make Calgary the envy of all the cities in North America. The centre would rise from where Chinatown now stands and would have a wonderful two-level bridge crossing the Bow whose course would be changed to form a huge lake around the $5 million city hall which was to be a miniature replica of the White House in Washington!

About the same time another Englishman, land developer John Hextall (of Hextall Home fame) came up with a plan to develop the Bow. He had the idea to develop a suburb, but he also needed to build a way across the river. Unaided by cost-sharing programs of senior governments, Hextall bore the entire cost of bridging the Bow. He soon realized, however, that his dream town was still not readily accessible to Calgary. So he completed a rather unusual agreement with the city in which he gave them two islands in the Bow River west of Calgary, the bridge and the Creek in exchange for streetcar service through his valley. The island became Bowness Park and the streetcar the most popular means of getting around for thousands of Calgarians without cars during the Depression.

On the east side of Hextall's bridge was the ranch of the family Shouldice after whom the bridge was later named. Roy Shouldice (82 years old when I talked with him) had a vivid memory of earlier days, "We called our ranch (or mixed farm, really) Shouldice Terrance. East of us was the farm of A. S. McKay – that's McKay Point today. Then east of them was the farm of Colonel Herchemer – that would be about where 16th Street N.W. is now."

Another early industry on the Bow banks was the Crandall Press Brick and Sandstone Company set up in 1905 at a railroad siding known as Shaganappi, about five miles west of the city limits at that time. One hundred brick makers and stone masons were soon producing up to 45 000 bricks per day for Calgary builders.

Roy Shouldice recollected, "Father and two hired men hauled the bricks across the frozen Bow to build our house high on the hill on the north side of the river in 1912." That house later became Calgary's crematorium.

Crandall's factories and workers' houses soon spread over 400 acres of the Edworth ranch and was the thriving community known as Brickburn until the First War. Then Depression and freight rates closed it down in 1931.

Edward Crandall's own brick mansion was built with two-foot thick walls and a walk-in vault, but after the close of the factory it was used for a time as a Red Cross

Children's hospital and in 1936 was bought by H. S. Patterson for under $2 000.

While Bowness and Montgomery grew toward Calgary in a sort of haphazard strip along its banks, the Bow flowed serenely on until 1963, when it suddenly became the centre of one of the greatest controversies ever to hit Calgary. The CPR proposed to build a railway line along the southern banks of the river throughout the heart of the city. Jack, then alderman, realizing not only the financial disaster of the proposed plan, but also the loss of the Bow riverbanks for citizen enjoyment, led an ultimately successful fight for two years to kill the CPR scheme.

Since that date citizen groups, such as Chief Justice McLaurin's Bow River Beautification Association, have contributed much time and money to assure continued public ownership of the Bow's riverbanks and in 1963 engineer Edgar H. Davis came up with the idea of an urban village. At that time there hadn't been an apartment block built in downtown Calgary for 30 years. But after many years of trying to rally financial support, Davis, like Kerr and Prince before him, eventually succeeded in developing his own project for the Bow river front that would have a positive impact for Calgary's growing community – Eau Claire market and apartments.

✳ ✳ ✳ ✳ ✳

# Monument to an Empire

*I* was in love when I first walked into the Burns Building in 1939. I was on my way to meet Jack's father for the first time. The old Burns Building appealed to me in my frame of mind, with its green and white marble foyer, marvellous marble staircase and handsome carved newel post. I could imagine its former grandeur.

The Leslie connection with the Burns Building goes back to the early 1920s when J. C. Leslie & Co. Realtors moved into an office where "Dad" Leslie remained for almost 30 years. There he was often visited by old timers like Percy Page and J. J. Bowler (both became lieutenant-governors) and farmers and ranchers like Slim Morehouse, who drove a 36 hitch of horses in the first Calgary Stampede Parade. Rents in the 1930s were $10 a month, and Jack remembers his father's outraged protest when rent for the Burns Building went up to $15. "That's a 50 percent increase!" he exploded. He was finally given more space to compensate for the higher rates.

During those "dirty thirties" real estate sales were few and far between, and every member of the Leslie family had to earn what he could, so Fridays after school Jack "peddled" *Liberty* and *The Saturday Evening Post* to the second-hand stores down the street, the nearby barber shop and in the basement of the Burns building itself, where there were always several customers to be found in the billiard parlor.

The real roots of the Burns Building go back to 1856 when Patrick Burns was born to immigrant Irish farmers in Oshawa, Ontario. The Burns family soon moved to Kirkfield, where Pat received a meagre education at the village school.

Pat moved to Winnipeg in 1878 and walked to his homestead at Minnedosa, where he soon became known as a personable Irishman who would seize any opportunity for honest work that would turn a dollar. It was in 1886 that he cashed in on a friendship begun on his first job, picking potatoes. There he had met an older boy, William Mackenzie, who was engaged in major railway construction in the state of Maine. Burns won a contract with him to supply meat for the building crews. A larger contract followed for construction camps along the railroad from Regina to Saskatoon and Prince Albert. Business almost ran away from Burns as he began supplying not only railroads but mining, construction and lumber camps.

When work began on the railway between Calgary and Edmonton, Burns set up headquarters in Calgary, operating from a shack on 9th Avenue East. Soon he had a packing plant and was supplying meat through more than 100 wholesale and retail outlets across Canada, from Saskatchewan to Vancouver Island and from Fort Macleod to Dawson City. It was said of Burns that he made a million dollars without losing a friend. By 1912 he owned 12 large cattle ranches, had retail meat markets in 27 towns and cities and operated two of the finest packing plants on the continent.

In 1911, the same year Thomas Mawson was drawing elaborate plans for a civic center, Pat Burns went ahead with his own statement of faith in Calgary's future – a magnificent six-storey business block at the corner of 8th avenue and 2nd Street East. It was completed early in 1913 and stood as one of the finest of its size in the whole West. It was a good example of the neo-classical building typical of the turn of the century. It was exceedingly striking and beautiful, faced with glazed white terra cotta and finished with massive and ornate cornices. Its construction was sound, built with reinforced concrete throughout and was "absolutely fireproof." It was fitted with the latest vacuum cleaning system, the best lighting, heating and ventilating systems that money and skill could provide. Electric power being somewhat sporadic in those days, natural gas was piped into each office for lighting purposes in addition to the electric wiring. There were four telephones in each office and a complete system of Cutler mail chutes running from the top storey to the bottom. Lavatories were on each floor, finished in tile and marble and each office had a marble basin with hot and cold water.

Burns and his architects Hodgson & Bates cleverly provided a comfortable outdoor shopping experience by protecting the sidewalk with the sloping glass canopy held by terra cotta lions. The ornamental iron scroll work and medallions along the canopy fringe were and still are, especially noteworthy, creating beautiful silhouette patterns. If you entered by the 8th Avenue entrance, you could walk up the marble stairs or take the Otis elevator (the fastest in the city) to the offices above. Or through a bay window to

*Burns building, meat market, c. 1913*

the left, people were beckoned into a market unequalled in Calgary's history.

It must have been like walking into a castle – twelve doric marble columns 25 feet high marched down the full length of a 130 foot-long hall. Beautiful chandeliers reminiscent of those found in old Norman castles hung from the high ceiling. The floors were, and still are, tiny hexagonal white ceramic tiles with a wide border of tiny black square tiles. The counters were all faced with beautiful green veined marble that climbed up to form part of the base of the columns. The counter tops were heavy glass, elegantly clipped to the marble with metal brackets (a marvellous "Italian influence"). Steam radiators were set in front of each marble column. At the far end of the hall was a real Western touch – a five-point elk's head mounted on the wall. Everything was ornate for a market. Even the refrigerator was set on marble pillars with P. Burns & Co. Ltd. Shamrock Brand and a drawing of a shamrock, etched into the plate glass window that fronted it.

On opening day potted ferns decorated every counter, behind which stood a long line of white-coated men, some behind butcher blocks, some behind stacks of cheese or in front of pickle barrels and pyramids of canned goods, others beside milk and dairy products. Giant scales stood in front of each butcher block indicating that Pat Burns must have expected large orders! Behind the butchers was an elaborate system of hangers and trolleys where carcasses could be rolled to and from the cold storage vault. A wire system carried money zinging along like a street car on a trolley line up to the office on the mezzanine floor where one or two cashiers could look after a whole floor of customers, and the "boss" could keep his eye on the entire operation through large windows with small leaded panes.

"We are renting the offices to a very high class of tenants," said the rental agents for the new building in 1913. But the First World War struck a year later and the bottom dropped out of Calgary's economy. Many of the 200 offices soon stood empty. Pat Burns' war efforts were plentiful. Food supplies to the Allies, food conservation campaigns at home, the donation of his sandstone mansion as an unofficial "government house" for visiting royalty and government dignitaries, and his support of many other charities all led to a popularity among the public that suggested he should run for public office and accept high honors. He refused the suggestion, but accepted two honors: one conferred by the Pope, and another by Freddie McCall. The intrepid flyer dropped a "bomb" containing an honorary membership to Calgary's Aero Club onto Burns' lawn!

Calgary and the country went all out on Pat Burns' 75th birthday in July 1931, which, coincidentally fell on the first day of that year's Stampede. Seven hundred dignitaries from all over North America attended a banquet at the Palliser Hotel. His 3 000 pound, three-tiered 7 ½ foot birthday cake was placed on the stage in front of the grandstand that evening with the 75 candles alight. It was an appropriate site, for Pat was one of the Big Four who had backed the first Stampede back in 1912. On that memorable evening, as he made the first cut in the cake, it was announced that he had accepted the senatorship offered by Prime Minister R. B. Bennett. Calgarians and vistors cheered as the cake was divided into 23 000 pieces and distributed to the public. Pat Burns died in 1937. His bequests covered every needy segment of Calgary's population.

In 1956, his beautiful mansion with its gardens occupying the entire block from 4th to 5th Streets West and from 12th to 13th Avenues, was demolished for it was said, "the house is too derelict to set aside for sentimental reasons." Through community effort, the Burns Building was saved from suffering a similar fate in 1979. Having survived, it remains a fitting legacy to a remarkable entrepreneur.

✳ ✳ ✳ ✳ ✳

# The First Stampede Queen

When Patsy Rodgers became the first Queen of the Calgary Exhibition and Stampede in 1946 she was simply following in her family's tradition of breaking new trails.

Her grandfather Dublin Rodgers, came from Ireland in 1883 and made his way to Alberta from Montana over the famous Benton Trail. Her grandparents on her mother's side sailed by schooner to San Francisco then followed overland trails to B.C. Her uncle was Johnny Hamilton, a stagecoach driver on the Cariboo Trail who later owned a Calgary livery stable. And her father was William Jasper (Jappy) Rodgers, who raised and trained polo ponies on the Virginia Ranch north of Cochrane. He also was a calf roper and worked with the rodeo livestock at the Calgary Stampede. That was the most important thing to teenaged Patsy. "I loved to ride around in the backfield on my pony. It was dusty and sweaty, but I'd watch the cowboys get ready for the rodeo events and then sit on the fence and root for my favorites."

When the Stampede Rodeo decided in 1946 it was time to have a Rodeo Queen to represent them at major rodeos in Texas and New York, the arena director Jack Dillon said he had just the right girl – Patsy, now Patti Henderson.

Riding in the 1946 Stampede Parade, she was thrust into a limelight she had never dreamed of. Through the shouting, cheering crowds and marching bands it was her excellent horsemanship that prepared her for the upcoming Lethbridge Rodeo.

In September, Patti flew to Fort Worth Texas, where she was joined by five other Rodeo Queens representing Southern States. "I was the only one from Canada. We drove from Fort Worth to Dublin, Texas to the Lightning C Ranch where we participated in a three-day rodeo. Then we traveled on a special rodeo train along with many contestants, their families and their horses to New York City. For seven evening performances and four matinees every week over five weeks we rode in the Grand Entry into Madison Gardens Square carrying our flags. I carried the old Red Ensign as the Stampede Board did not yet have its own flag. We also made guest appearances throughout New York at sporting events, rode in downtown parades, and visited veterans hospitals with movie cowboy Gene Autry and his horse Champion . . . this was the heyday of the great cowboy singers."

The Queens were also chaperoned. "Don't think they didn't watch," Patti laughs. "One night we decided to duck out down the fire escape to meet some cowboys who were taking us to see the original Ink Spots. We were caught. If it hadn't been so near the end of the show we would have been sent home."

Patti's triumphant southern tour convinced the Stampede Board that a Queen was an excellent goodwill ambassador. At that time many Calgary community clubs supported their activities with Queen contests where tickets were sold for each contestant. Associated Canadian Travelers suggested a similar scheme on this idea to the Stampede Board and the city-wide Stampede Queen contests were born.

Although this was a good fund-raiser, sometimes there were grumbling of unfairness as the daughter of a wealthy and benevolent father could win more easily by buying up tickets – and she might not even be able to ride a horse!

In 1964 the Stampede Board set up a volunteer committee to select judges and make up contest rules. The committee emphasized that it was "definitely not a cheesecake competition." The girl must have an appeal – a fresh young face to set the tone for the year. They are also judged on public speaking ability and equestrian skills, and have to be able to work with people on a one-on-one basis and with a large crowd.

Former Stampede Queens and Princesses are scattered around the globe, but the ones who live in the Calgary area continue with volunteer work for the Stampede through their Queen's Alumni Association Committee formed in 1980. The first chairperson was Wayne Chisholm with Patti Henderson serving as secretary. She later moved up to vice-chairperson and finally to chairperson. This committee of Queens and Princesses hosts the Annual Stampede Special, a free pancake breakfast and morning on the midway for all Calgary's handicapped children.

In 1984, Patti, the first Stampede Queen was given a lifetime appointment as *Special Honorary Associate of the Calgary Exhibition and Stampede* in recognition of 42 years of participation in the Greatest Outdoor Show on Earth.

*Patti Henderson*

*née*

*Patsy Rodgers*

\*\*\*\*\*

# Western Hospitality

*I*n 1967 Heads of State making official visits to celebrate Canada's Centennial were obliged to pay their respects in Ottawa but from there the dignitaries were allowed to visit one other city of their choice. Many chose Calgary because they had heard about the Calgary Stampede. The problem was that Stampede lasted only a short time that year (nine days) while VIP visits extended over several months. Mayor Leslie's solution, like that of earlier mayors, was to escort them to a hospitable foothills ranch. In 1896 mayors like William Cushing and James Reilly drove their guests such as Lord and Lady Minto and Sir Charles Napier out to the R. G. Robinson Ranch seven kilometers from Fort Calgary. Guests were driven out to the ranch in the smartest equipage, with the best horse teams available and escorted by a detail of the North West Mounted Police. While there they enjoyed Mrs. Robinson's "whole-souled" hospitality, and were entertained by a rodeo featuring bucking and roping of wild horses and steers.

The Robinsons had come from San Francisco in 1888. Mrs. Robinson almost lost her courage her first October here when she found herself with a new baby in a crude, chinked log cabin with snow drifting in during an early winter storm. But they persevered and soon had a new house and a large horse ranch that did business with big ranchers and entrepreneurs like Pat Burns, who paid a very decent price for a pair of grey geldings. They also supplied horses and farrier services to the North West Mounted Police. The Robinson's Elbow Park Ranch be-

113

came a favorite spot for Calgarians. Old timers insisted that the hospitality of the ranch was unequaled and that Mrs. Robinson was one of the finest women in the country. No wonder! She often entertained 20 or 30 for luncheon or dinner, so word must have gotten around quickly. The Robinson ranch now lies at the bottom of Glenmore Lake.

*The Robinson Family on their ranch, Mr. and*

*Mrs. Robinson on the porch, c. 1894*

However Western hospitality was as warm as ever at Twin Rivers Ranch where Jack took some of Calgary's VIPs during his term as mayor. Long, sleek black limousines, loaned out for the occasion, were now our "best equipage." But we were still accompanied by a Royal Canadian Mounted Police escort and enjoyed a special rodeo show.

Our hosts, and owners of the Two Rivers Ranch, were Ken and "Tiny" Paget. "Tiny" was Mrs. Paget's nickname because she was just four foot nine, but a bundle of energy. The Pagets in 1957 purchased 3 300 acres of gently rolling ranchland tucked into the hills halfway between Calgary and Banff. There, overlooking the Bow and Ghost Rivers, amid dogwood, fir and poplar trees they built an indoor arena with barns and stables. They specialized in horse breeding, one being the world famous quarterhorse stallion King Leo Bar, the horse could do practically anything well and was one of the top ten stallions in North America for breeding. They also built a large ranch house where a warm atmosphere of friendliness pervaded the air, the kind of hospitality the West was and still is famous for.

Jack and his Council first went to the Pagets in June of 1967 with His Excellency Dr. Heinrich Luebke, President of the Federal Republic of Germany. Security for him was tighter than any we had experienced with other guests. Someone told me that the young father rocking a baby carriage at the airport was in fact a police officer and when Luebke went to Banff all side roads were blocked off until he had passed. Even though it was then 22 years since the end of WWII there was still the fear that someone might seek revenge. President Luebke was a gentle-faced, grand-fatherly-looking man with snow white hair. He showed a keen interest in the stock and the ranch operations. The Pagets, their children and ranch hands put on a magnificent rodeo for us. At the ranch, his white hair blowing from under his white Calgary hat, President Luebke explored the hills behind the Paget ranch house. He also visited the Highland Stock Farm of Don and Jean Matthews where Don, a former president of the Calgary Stampede had a large prize herd of Aberdeen-Angus cattle. He also saw the John Copithorne Dairy Farm at Cochrane because it was considered to be one of the typical dairy farms of Alberta. President Luebke, as a former Minister of Agriculture, was very interested in both.

In October 1967 we went again to the Paget Ranch – this time with Lieutenant General Ankrah, head of the African State of Ghana. Ankra deposed his predecessor and turned Ghana from socialism and Russian domination toward free enterprise and closer connections with the West. His interest in Canada was sparked by a Canadian Armed Forces training team which had been sent to Ghana to help train the Ghana soldiers. He was most anxious to have Ken Paget and western technicians come to his country to show them how to operate their pre-stress cement plants which the Communists had built under Nkruma but had left without operators. Ken Paget introduced ready-mix concrete to Calgary to speed up Calgary's post-war building boom, and later came up with a concept of instant packaged "pre-stress bridges," many of which span the rivers of the trans-Canada highway.

For General Ankrah's visit Ken Paget gave General and Mrs. Ankrah colorful Hudson Bay coats and of course the whole party had on their City of Calgary white hats. Although I'll never know what problems Mrs. Robinson encountered while entertaining VIPs in her day, I do know how Mrs. Paget felt on this occassion – panic stricken! She had the luncheon all organized with the well-known and dependable Calgary caterer Bessie Emm. Suddenly, late the day before, Jack's secretary, Kay Wood, phoned Tiny to say the count for the number of guests had been revised from 100 to 132! With naiveté born of the freedom we enjoy in our democracy, no one had thought to include the military dictator's ever-present retinue, 32 of them, and most were security men! Tiny already had a huge roast of beef but decided she had better order 12 pounds more. Fortunately she took the 20 pounds her butcher happened to have all cut and ready to go.

As for the meal Tiny described, "They dug in with appetites that would have done credit to a Canadian threshing crew!" The General himself sent Tiny scurrying to the cupboard for everything peppery she could find, and he smothered that beautiful Alberta roast beef with condiments like Tobasco, Worchestershire Sauce and Liquid Smoke. He also declined a special chocolate roll with rum sauce and asked for fresh fruit, completely unaware that in Alberta, fruit in October is not exactly plentiful. But I wouldn't want to give the impression that the Ghanians were difficult guests. On the contrary, they were delightful. It was unfortunate that before the Canadians got to Ghana to help them, General Ankra had himself been deposed.

However his security held while he was in Calgary except for one incident for which they were caught unprepared. The wife of one of Calgary's aldermen (with the help of good wine) became overly enthusiastic in her desire to show Canadian good-will to our visitor. Unexpectedly she sat upon the General's knee, threw her arms around his neck and said, "General, I think you're jus' wunerful!" Whereupon the guard with the sawed-off shot gun strapped to his pant leg, looked at the guard with the shoulder pistol holster and shrugged helplessly.

Canadians can be pretty blasé about visiting dignitaries, but the Canadian Centennial in 1967 seemed to inspire in Canadians a new kind of love and pride in themselves. It made it easier for us able to show some of that love to our VIPs. I think old ranchers like the Robinsons would have said, "Those Calgarians are still our kind of people."

\* \* \* \* \*

# *On Our Best Royal Behavior*

When Princess Alexandra paid her official visit to present the Guidon pennant to the South Alberta Light Horse and the Colours to the Calgary Highlanders on May 24th, 1967, the weather turned to a downpour and so windy it took two militiamen to carry each standard.

I have never seen so many looking so miserable with the cold. However like captains standing on the bridge of a sinking ship, unflinching in the gail-like wind stood Princess Alexandra and Honorary Colonel Sam Nickle for one long hour. She was dressed elegantly in a light weight turquoise coat over a sleeveless, cream wool dress because, she said, "From my window at the Palliser the slate grey sky didn't look much worse than any average London day. Nobody told me about the wind." Sam Nickle, 80 years of age and just five feet tall, was dressed in a dark grey business suit because he did not have a proper Army issue overcoat.

A Calgary wind will chill your bones to the marrow, turn your blood to ice and your nose into a dripping tap. But when you are taking a Brigade salute you must stand rigidly at attention. You may rock back and forth slightly on your heels or imperceptibly flex your knees to keep from falling on your face, but get a hanky from your pocket? Never. The Princess saw Sam's dilemma and whispered out of the side of her mouth, "Use your sleeve."

Finally the wretched hour passed. The Princess was whisked off to review the freezing troops in an army vehicle which looked like a direct descendant of a Ben Hur chariot. At last the ceremony was over and the smiling princess walked along the parade square shaking hands with school children. One more salute and Sam and the princess both left the dias, bending their brittle bodies into a waiting Cadillac.

Quipped Sam Nickle, "That's the only time I ever got under a blanket with a princess!"

*Princess Alexandra, 1967*

✳ ✳ ✳ ✳ ✳

# The Military Connection

$A$t a July, 1994 Stampede breakfast, held on a sunny hill overlooking Heritage Park, I met Lieutenant Colonel Ray Wlasichuck, Commanding Officer of the Lord Strathcona Royal Canadians Battle Group who was home on a short leave from Bosnia. Meeting him brought back memories of what I remember as "the military connection" with the City of Calgary.

It was R. B. Bennett who decreed Calgary should have Currie Barracks, which were finished in 1936 along with an adjacent temporary military airport. Built on the western edge of the city, the Sarcee Barracks were completed in 1958. In 1968 it was renamed Harvey Barracks and joined to Currie to form the Canadian Forces Base, Calgary. The Base is not only one of the largest employers in Calgary but is a proud presence that reminds us of the sacrifices which have been made and are still being made to keep our freedom.

The large size of the military base (15 000 in 1967), visits of military VIPs such as Lord Louis Mountbatten and ceremonies such as Freedom of the City parades, means that most Calgary mayors have been involved with this important community. One ceremony I remember Jack and I attending was the First Battalion Princess Patricia's Canadian Light Infantry requesting the "freedom of the city." The battalion formed up in front of City Hall and the City Marshall, Colonel D. G. H. Cunnington placed himself at the foot of the city hall steps and said, "Who comes here?"

Colonel A.M. Potts, Commanding Officer, replied, "The first Battalion Princess Patricia's Canadian Light Infantry requesting the ancient privilege and right to march through the city with drums beating, bayonets fixed and colors flying."

*Mayor Leslie bids farewell to the Queen's Own Rifle,*

*June 7, 1968*

While the officers retired into City Hall the soldiers stood, eyes front, shoulders stiff, every limb trembling with rigid attention, waiting for the inspection. Colonel Hutchinson, sitting next to me on the reviewing stand suddenly (without moving even his head) said, "Sergeant your number one man in the second row right." As my eyes swung around I saw the man turn purple, gasp and, body rigid as a flagpole, fall flat on his face. He was immediately laid behind the lines while an ambulance was called. Army discipline is such that the inspection went on as though nothing had happened. Colonel Cunnington led Colonel Potts and Jack to the front of the battalion where, after a short speech he said, "Take advantage of the privilege granted to you in 1952 of making a war-like appearance in the City of Calgary with drums beating, bayonets fixed and colors flying." After the customary three cheers for the mayor the battalion swung off to the Regimental March which would bring them to a saluting dias in front of The Bay. There Jack was to be in position to take the salute. Unfortunately the military driver, unfamiliar with downtown streets, took a wrong turn which put us behind the troops. Zig-zagging down back lanes he finally picked up a motor-cycle escort that got us there in time, albeit with frazzled nerves.

Another connection I remember fondly was the 2nd Battalion Queen's Own. They were closer to our hearts than most regiments for we had seen them off at the airport when they left for peacekeeping duties in Cyprus in April 1967. Most of us take for granted the service of these NATO troops and forget the heartache of separation they and their families suffer. Not long after they left Jack was officiating at the opening of the Spring Bull Sale. "I saw a particularly fine steer and startled everyone by bidding on it – and getting my bid! That was one of the few things I did without waiting for council approval. When it became known that I wanted to send the beef to the men in Cyprus, Arthur Childs (president of P. Burns & Co.) offered to dress the animal and arrange for shipping."

On October 16, 1967 we were there on the tarmac when a big RCAF Yukon plane dropped out of the morning sky to return 125 men from Cyprus, the final contingent of the 2nd Battalion Queen's Own. The troops and officers walking down the ramp tried to look absolutely professional and unemotional but their eyes darted through the crowd looking for their loved ones. Colonel Robinson, the commanding officer, saluted the Calgary Base Commander, shook hands Jack and other dignitaries, shook hands with me and then stood in front of his wife. He paused a split second, then leaned over and kissed her. Mrs. Robinson laughed and whispered, "For a minute, I thought he was going to shake hands with me too!"

A year later Jack received a large pair of bull's horns mounted on a plaque which reads, *"Presented to His Worship Mayor Jack Leslie in appreciation of your active interest in the Second Battalion. In Cyprus that gift of Western beef made Calgary Day, August 1, 1967 a day to remember . . . Queen's Own Rifles of Canada."* According to Captain Bill Guscott much of the beef in Cyprus was from Yugoslavia and as tough as shoe leather. Not only was the Calgary beef tender but the taste brought back memories from home. It was a sad day when in June of 1968 the 2nd Battalion Queen's Own Rifles of Canada was disbanded (or as in army parlance, "put to nil strength"). This event also merited a Freedom of the City Ceremony but on that day there were 108 all ranks, a figure symbolic of the number of years of unbroken service to Canada.

The military connection is yet again being weakened. Ottawa announced in June 1994 that the Lord Strathcona Horse will be moved to Edmonton by the summer of 1996. This can hardly be considered a Centennial gift. A walk into the Officer's Mess of the Strathcona's is like a walk back in time, with its flags, pennants and honors of the battalion displaying the battles hard won by our soldiers. A valuable piece of Calgary history will be lost if this costly and unnecessary move goes forward.

✳ ✳ ✳ ✳ ✳

# What Goes Up Must Come Down

$M$y husband became Mayor of Calgary in 1965 and being a conscientious soul, had by 1967 performed many unusual public relations duties to promote the city. Some were hazardous, such as walking around the still unfinished platform of the 600 foot Calgary Tower, and although I had known for months that he was to take part in the Canadian Centennial International Balloon Event, like Scarlett O'Hara I said to myself, "I'll worry about that tomorrow."

It wasn't until the bright sunny day of July 7th when I went down to the Infield of the CalgaryExhibition and Stampede to watch the ascent, that the full impact of the impending event hit me. Now in 1994 no one would think anything of it, for Calgarians can look skyward almost any given day and see 10 or even 20 hot air balloons soaring over the city. But in 1967 only the odd one had been flown in Canada before. These were not the hot air balloons of today.

There towered *Spelterini* looking like some prehistoric monster, her orange and silver sides swollen to a 30 foot girth with 1 200 cubic metres of helium and suspended from her belly, a tiny four by four rattan basket.

"My husband is going up in *that*?" I groaned. While the sport had long been popular in Europe, less than a dozen Canadians up to that time had ever flown helium-filled balloons. The Committee rushed me over to meet Pilot

Fred Dolder, the legendary balloonist from Zurich, Switzerland. He and his wife insisted that ballooning is safe as churches, and that a balloon is built with everything fifteen times as strong as it needs to be. Mercifully they skipped tales I later heard of balloons landing on chimneys and bursting into flames or floating against high-tension electric cables and exploding.

*Herr* Dolder, a large man already in his late sixties with keen, smiling blue eyes and a trim, snow-white beard and his kindly wife were such honest-looking folk that they inspired confidence as they explained the simple technique of the sport. The fabric bag of the balloon is contained by a network of ropes, the ends of which are attached to a wooden or steel ring. The basket is reinforced with steel cables and dangles from the ring and weighed down with sandbags. The helium-filled bag becomes lighter than the air around it. Jettison enough excess ballast (sand) and the balloon floats off. Release some gas and it descends. The valve through which the gas is released is a simple wooden disc fixed in a frame in the top of the balloon and held closed by rubber or steel springs. It is worked by a string which dangles through the middle of the balloon, out through a tiny sleeve in the bottom and down into the basket. An airplane moves up and down by means of elaborate and expensive machinery, the balloon can be worked by string and sand.

Getting the ballast right for launching is a painstakingly slow process. On this occasion the ground crew consisted of members of the Princess Patricia's Canadian Light Infantry Brigade, each standing with their two hands on the basket, hand to hand all around the rim waiting until Mr. Dolder shouted "Release." They let go for just a second and it started to rise until he yelled "Hold." He scooped a few handsfull of sand out of the bags and again called "Release." Almost immediately he shouted "Hold." This went on over and over again until he felt that the ballast was just right to get him and his crew off the ground.

I think it must be pretty tricky to judge when your passengers are of various shapes and weights. In this case they were – co-pilot Vic Kavan (then President of the Canadian Balloon Club), Chuck Rathgeb (well-known Toronto sportsman) each weighing somewhere around 180 pounds; John Fisher (Canada's Centennial Commissioner) at 200 pounds and Jack Leslie at 160 pounds.

*A balloon ride for Canada's centennial, 1967*

Finally, brandishing on high a bottle of champagne and a roll of toilet paper, Dolder ordered his crew aboard. He went through the *release – hold* routine once more and just as I thought he was going to repeat it, suddenly they soared up into the air so fast I couldn't even snap a picture before they were out of range.

Jack was an experienced airplane pilot but he said later the sensation was unlike anything he had ever known before – a Mary Poppins sort of feeling. As they slid steadily upward the infield dropped softly away, the Calgary Stampede grandstand and all its thousands shrank into toy-sized miniatures. And the silence – the beautiful, peaceful silence.

Most people think of air as a simple static mass but it is constantly in motion, flowing, twisting, rising and falling. A balloon does not move *through* the air but *in* it, like a log moving down a river. The trick is to shift the balloon up and down to find the best air currents.

The group had been warned that it didn't matter where they drifted as long as it wasn't over McCall Field – so where did they drift? Right over that International airfield! Not only did they drift there they stayed there. Suddenly the air currents just didn't move them and I can imagine the stunned look on the face of any jet pilot who glanced out his window to see crazy balloonists to his portside.

Thankfully they were soon on the move and sailed to the North and West where the foothills took on a totally different view from that which you get from an airplane. The world is not flat – the hills and valleys roll infront of the spectator.

With toilet paper fluttering to give the wind direction, Mr. Dolder suddenly popped the cork on the champagne. "We have a custom among balloonists," he smiled, "when you have passed your first hour in the air you become one of us," and he splashed a bit of the bubbly on each person's head.

As the foothills grew closer, *Herr* Dolder decided it was time to come down, but as they descended his fluttering toilet paper told him they were running into extra strong ground currents – therein lay the makings of disaster.

He began releasing gas from the balloon in small spurts until...you remember the valve I mentioned that worked by the string dangling into the basket... it stuck! Instead of the gentle bump they had been promised they landed with a thud something like being pushed off a speeding truck.

"Then," chuckled Jack, "We rocketed into the blue sky, then thump back down and up again. I called to Dolder 'Should I jump out next time we land and hold the basket down?' But the Swiss gentleman in his excitement reverted to his native tongue which I didn't understand. I jumped anyway, next time we hit 'terra firma' but the wind caught us and up went *Spelterini*."

Laughed John Fisher later, "There was Jack, the Mayor of Calgary dangling from her side!"

*Herr* Dolder scrambled onto the shoulders of John Fisher and reached the stuck valve; the bag emptied, the balloon fell quickly to the ground and the basket spilled its three large occupants upon Jack's prostrate form.

It is doubtful that any bronc at the Calgary Stampede gave his cowboy as rough a landing as the balloon *Spelterini* gave its riders.

✳ ✳ ✳ ✳ ✳